I0805244

CHILDREN'S MATHEMATICS
COGNITIVELY GUIDED INSTRUCTION

GUIDE FOR WORKSHOP LEADERS

ELIZABETH FENNEMA
University of Wisconsin–Madison

THOMAS P. CARPENTER
University of Wisconsin–Madison

LINDA LEVI
University of Wisconsin–Madison

MEGAN LOEF FRANKE
University of California–Los Angeles

SUSAN B. EMPSON
University of Texas–Austin

HEINEMANN • PORTSMOUTH, NH

NCTM

Heinemann

361 Hanover Street
Portsmouth, NH 03801-3912
www.heinemann.com

The National Council of Teachers of Mathematics
1906 Association Drive
Reston, VA 22091-1593

Offices and agents throughout the world

The development of the CGI Professional Development Program was supported in part by the National Science Foundation under Grant Numbers MDR-8955346 and MDR-8550236. The opinions expressed are those of the authors and do not necessarily reflect the views of the National Science Foundation.

A set of seven videotapes illustrating the ideas presented in this book can be ordered from the Wisconsin Center for Education Research. The tapes supplement the CDs included with the book of readings for workshop participants, *Children's Mathematics: Cognitively Guided Instruction*. The seven videotapes include ninety-three examples of individual children solving problems and ten classroom episodes with accompanying teacher commentary. One tape provides an overview of CGI including comments from the authors and from teachers who have participated in the program. To order the tapes, contact:

Center Document Service, Room 242
Wisconsin Center for Education Research
1025 W. Johnson St.
Madison, WI 53706
Phone: (608) 265-9698

Stock #00861

Editor: Leigh Peake
Production: Melissa L. Inglis
Cover design: Darci Mehall
Manufacturing: Louise Richardson

15 14 VP 12 13 14 15

To Deborah Carey

CONTENTS

Preface vii

Acknowledgments viii

Introduction ix

Getting Started: Introducing Cognitively Guided Instruction 1

Reflections on Teaching Chapter 1: "Children's Mathematical Thinking" 3

Reflections on Teaching Chapter 2: "Addition and Subtraction: Problem Types" 5

Reflections on Teaching Chapter 3: "Addition and Subtraction: Children's Solution Strategies" 11

Reflections on Teaching Chapter 4: "Multiplication and Division: Problem Types and Children's Solution Strategies" 15

Reflections on Teaching Chapter 5: "Problem Solving as Modeling" 18

Reflections on Teaching Chapter 6: "Multidigit Number Concepts" 19

Reflections on Teaching Chapter 7: "Beginning to Use Cognitively Guided Instruction" 23

Reflections on Teaching Chapter 8: "CGI Classrooms" 25

Appendix A: Sample Workshop Agendas 29

Appendix B: Problems and Worksheets 41

Appendix C: Getting Started Questions 55

Appendix D: Selected Annotated Bibliography 59

PREFACE

For the last decade, with National Science Foundation support, primary-school teachers and mathematics educators from the University of Wisconsin–Madison have been working together to learn how to assist teachers to use research-based knowledge about children's thinking in classrooms. Cognitively Guided Instruction (CGI) is the result of this collaboration. Our suggestions are based on research carried out over a decade by staff as well as outside researchers. This research has been reported in other sources. CGI has been evaluated extensively and modified in accordance with what research has indicated and it has been shown to be effective in many diverse situations.

CGI is not a typical primary-school mathematics program. Rather, it is a professional development program in which teachers learn to assess children's thinking in mathematics and to use what they know about children's thinking during instruction. The CGI Professional Development Program is a series of workshops in which participants initially learn about a structured framework of mathematics and children's thinking and the ways children's thinking evolves. Participants learn by watching, discussing, and reflecting upon children solving mathematical problems. Participants assess the validity of the framework as they work with their own students and learn to take their students' thinking into consideration as they make instructional decisions. Resulting CGI classrooms have critical components in common, but the classrooms are also unique because each teacher decides how s/he will use children's thinking in his/her classroom.

The material to support implementing a CGI Professional Development Program includes

- A book of readings for workshop participants titled *Children's Mathematics: Cognitively Guided Instruction*, a copy of which accompanies this Guide. These readings were developed from the research-based framework of children's thinking in mathematics.
- Reflections on leading workshops (contained in this Guide), including suggestions for implementing a Professional Development Program, a selected annotated bibliography, and a selection of resources such as sample workshop agendas and worksheets.
- Seven videotapes illustrating children's thinking and a variety of CGI classrooms in action. The videotapes are available separately from the University of Wisconsin by contacting the Center Document Service, Room 242; Wisconsin Center for Education Research; 1025 W. Johnson St.; Madison, WI 53706; (608) 265-9698.

It is expected that this *Guide for Workshop Leaders* will be used by individuals who have participated in a CGI Professional Development Program and have worked with children in CGI classrooms.

ACKNOWLEDGMENTS

A very special thanks to Penelope Peterson. Without her, Cognitively Guided Instruction would never have existed.

Our thanks for many faithful, intelligent, and hardworking staff members at the Wisconsin Center for Education Research at the University of Wisconsin–Madison, who made significant contributions to CGI: Lisa Byrd Adajian, Rebecca Ambrose, Ellen Ansell, Jae-Meen Baek, Jeanie Behrends, Laura Brinker, Deborah A. Carey, P. L. Chiang, Donald Chambers, Rosemary Griffin, Janice Gratch, Judith Hankes, Eric Gutstein, Richard Lehrer, Victoria Jacobs, Cheryl Lubinski, Gregory Thoyre, and Janet Warfield.

Our thanks and appreciation are also extended to those who offered help in the development of this Guide: Fae Dremock, Chris Kruger, Margie Pligge, Sydney Raynal, Kay Schultz, and Nancy Vacc.

Many teachers and their students have contributed to the development of CGI. We cannot possibly list all of their names, but the following provided direct help or have been directly quoted or shown in this Guide or the accompanying book of readings for workshop participants:

Ann Badeau
Jennifer Beard
Lynn Behrendt
Sue Berthouex
Mary Bostrom
Kerri Burkey
Cathy Chenoweth
Karen Falkner
Joan Fleming
Brenda Fujikawa
Michelle Garden
Susan Gehn
Almeta Hawkins
Mazie Jenkins
Margaret Jenson
Annie Keith
Virginia Koberstein
Therese Kolan
Barbara Martin
Craig Meyer
Candy Nerge
Mary Paquette
Patricia Rentschler
Kathy Statz
Ruth Steiner
Ken Swift
Francine Tate
Pam Thomas
Carrie Valentine
Dyanne Van Den Heuvel
Barbara Wiesner
Mary Jo Yttri

INTRODUCTION

> CGI is a way of teaching math that looks at how children solve problems on their own, without your assistance. That's your starting point. To get to know them, what they can do all by themselves, their own way. And then you make decisions about where you would like the children to go next.
>
> Jennifer Beard, first-grade teacher

> A CGI classroom is where you build on the math knowledge of your children according to what they know. . . . You don't build objectives that say they should be doing this, this, this, and this. You sort of take what they know and build on from there.
>
> Susan Gehn, first- and third-grade teacher

> CGI is a philosophy versus a recipe. . . . You as a teacher have to take the knowledge that CGI is about problem types, about solution strategies, about how children develop cognitively, and you have to apply that to your own teaching style.
>
> Mazie Jenkins, first-grade teacher

The above statements by Cognitively Guided Instruction (CGI) teachers emphasize the importance of basing mathematics instruction on children's thinking. During the CGI Professional Development Program, CGI teachers develop an understanding of a research-based framework that helps them learn more about their students' thinking and supports them as they decide how best to apply what they have learned.

> It takes extra work . . . [to] know about this group of students or this particular student and [say] what I am going to do now that I know that. And I think it puts a lot of responsibility on the teacher to make a good judgment, for what's best for the class, what's best for this particular child.
>
> Brenda Fujikawa, third-grade teacher

The research-based framework of children's thinking in addition, subtraction, multiplication, and division with single- and multidigit numbers (presented in Chapters 1–6 of *Children's Mathematics*) describes how this thinking evolves. Knowledge of this framework makes it easier for teachers to assess whether or not children understand the mathematics they are asked to learn and to select problems that help children's thinking develop.

UNDERSTANDING MATHEMATICS

> It is only when you build from within that you really understand something. If children don't build from within and you just try to explain it to a child then it's not really learned. It is only rote, and that's not really understanding.
>
> Ann Badeau, second-grade teacher

> In the past I thought children didn't understand subtraction with regrouping, when what they didn't understand was how to use the process that I was insisting that they use, rather than really understanding the concept of subtraction that might encompass regrouping.
>
> Kerri Burkey, second-grade teacher

When children understand something, they can use that knowledge in numerous ways, they remember it longer, and they can use it to learn more mathematics. To understand means to be able to see relationships. For example, consider how Sheila (a first grader) used relationships when she solved the following problem:

> *Jerry had 8 balloons. Sue gave him 7 more balloons. How many balloons does Jerry have?*
>
> *Sheila*: 15
>
> *Teacher*: How did you know that?
>
> *Sheila*: Well, 8 and 8 are 16, so I knew that 8 and 7 was 1 less and that is 15.

Sheila related the numbers in the problem to the addition facts she already knew. She understood the mathematics behind the problem. We know that when we understand something we remember it and are better able to use that understanding in a variety of ways. This is also true for children.

All children have informal or intuitive knowledge that can serve as the basis for developing understanding of the formal mathematics of the curriculum. Children in CGI classes solve a large variety of problems involving addition, subtraction, multiplication, and division with single- and multidigit numbers. Teachers pose problems, each child decides how to solve the problems, and the solutions are shared with peers and teacher. The various solutions are discussed and then the entire process is repeated. As children solve many problems, reflect upon what they have done, and discuss their solutions, their intuitive knowledge of mathematics develops and is extended.

> They're learning to think. They're understanding what they're doing and not just computing. They're learning to explain how they're thinking, which is a lot different from what we used to do. All those things are happening as they add and subtract and multiply and divide and use fractions and use money and time and all that.
>
> Ruth Steiner, first-grade teacher

ROLE OF THE TEACHER

> We have learned to gear our instruction towards what the children know and what they are thinking rather than trying to push a certain method down the children's throats as far as how they are to learn to do math. They come up with their own ideas, and you just branch off from that. I'm a decision maker.
>
> Ann Badeau, second-grade teacher

CGI teachers do not tell children how to solve problems. However, they actively make decisions that enable children to use their knowledge to solve increasingly difficult problems. Experienced CGI teachers believe that they need to find out what children know and then use that knowledge to enable each child's knowledge of mathematics to mature. When one teacher was asked to describe her role and how she implemented it, she said,

> It's to watch the kids to see what they're doing, to see how they're thinking, and to try to challenge them. My role is just helping. Not showing them how, but giving them different opportunities and stretching them as they go.
>
> Ruth Steiner, first-grade teacher

Although these teachers believed that children could solve problems on their own and should be encouraged to use their own solution strategies, these teachers did not perceive their role to be passive. They believed their role was to understand their students' thinking and then actively to make decisions about what experiences those children should have to ensure that their knowledge and abilities in mathematics grew.

> I try to capitalize on the things that they actually know and can bring to the class. A kid might just come up to me and say, "I know what 15 and 15 is." And then I'd ask them how they did that, and they would tell me. And then when they're solving another problem and they go back to their old way of doing it, I might say to them, "Well, I remember when you said to me that 15 and 15 was 30, and then you told me that was 10 and 5 and 10 and 5, so you put those 10s together." And then I sort of say, "Look at these numbers in the new problem. Is there a way that you might use some of what you did before to solve the new one?"
>
> Sue Berthouex, first-grade teacher

Cognitively Guided Instruction is a way of teaching mathematics that enables children to solve many problems in any way they choose, thereby supporting the development of their mathematical understanding and skills. CGI teachers learn to understand children's thinking and are therefore able to teach mathematics in a way that encourages the growth of each child's understanding of mathematics.

COMMON COMPONENTS OF CGI CLASSROOMS

CGI does not prescribe the scope and sequence of the mathematics to be taught. Neither does it provide instructional materials for children, nor suggest that there is an optimal way to organize a class for instruction. Instead, the learning experiences of the CGI Professional Development Program are structured so that teachers learn a research-based model of children's mathematical thinking that helps them understand their own students' thinking. Teachers then must decide how to use that knowledge to make instructional decisions.

As each teacher implements and refines plans, a unique CGI classroom emerges, structured to fit his/her teaching style, knowledge, beliefs, and students. However, these unique classrooms have the following common components:

- Problem solving is the focus of instruction; teachers pose a variety of problems.
- Many problem-solving strategies are used to solve problems. Children decide how they should solve each problem.
- Children communicate to their teachers and peers how they solved the problems.

- Teachers understand children's problem-solving strategies and use that knowledge to plan instruction.

There are several *basic assumptions* about children's learning of mathematics that are reflected in CGI classrooms.

- Children have knowledge of mathematics, which should be used as a basis for instructional decisions.
- Children develop mathematical understanding and acquire skills by solving a variety of problems in any way that they choose.
- Children gain understanding and inform other children and their teachers as they communicate their mathematical thinking.

THE PROFESSIONAL DEVELOPMENT PROGRAM

The Professional Development Program reflects the basic assumptions about children's learning that are the foundation of CGI.

- Teachers' understanding of their students' thinking enables them to make instructional decisions. This, in turn, enables their students to learn with understanding.
- Teachers have intuitive understandings of children's thinking that can serve as the basis for acquiring a more structured understanding of children's thinking.
- Teachers can understand the thinking of each child in their classroom when they have a structured understanding of children's thinking.
- Teaching for understanding is too complex to be prescribed. Thus, teaching is a process of problem solving. The problem solving that teachers must do in order to encourage their students to learn with understanding is facilitated by knowledge of children's thinking, by communication with other teachers about their students' problem solving, and by working with children in classrooms.

The Professional Development Program, designed to enable participants to develop a structured understanding of children's thinking, consists of a series of workshops accompanied by work in classrooms with children. In the workshops, teachers interact with the CGI model of children's thinking as portrayed by solution-strategy frameworks (see Chapters 1–6 in *Children's Mathematics*). The workshops start with teachers' preexisting knowledge about children's thinking and continue by aiding teachers to build a structured body of knowledge that enables them to understand the thinking of each child in the classroom.

The workshops and work in classrooms are closely integrated. While teachers are gaining formal knowledge about children's thinking in the workshops, they work directly with students in their classrooms by asking them to solve problems and talk about their solution strategies. What they find out from their own students is discussed in the workshops in relation to what other teachers have learned and in relation to the research-based model of children's thinking.

The Model of Children's Thinking

The model of children's thinking presented here is derived from a substantial body of research done over the last several decades. This research is composed of specific mathematical concepts characterized by certain types of word problems and children's solution strategies for these word problems. The model that provides the impetus for teachers to develop their own understanding of children's thinking is described thoroughly in Chapters 1–6 of the readings for workshop participants. It is organized around a few overarching principles that enable an extensive range of problem types and solution strategies to be understood.

THE PEDAGOGY OF THE WORKSHOPS

Teaching is both an art and a science. Leading a workshop requires a similar art and a great deal of science. Enabling teachers to learn current knowledge about children's thinking should be the main activity of the workshops. The readings (*Children's Mathematics*) provide the science for the workshops. This Guide is designed to help you develop the art of leading a workshop through the reflections of other CGI leaders, participants, and researchers.

Essential Knowledge for Leaders

Many people have led CGI workshops, and although there are common themes and emphases, there is also variation in what has been done to help teachers to learn to use CGI in their classrooms. The backgrounds of successful leaders have been varied, but they have shared two common characteristics. The first is a thorough understanding of the research-based model of children's thinking. This understanding cannot be acquired unless you have worked extensively with children—asking them to solve problems, listening to their solutions, and acquiring an understanding of the model in relation to specific children.

The second is that successful workshop leaders have either been CGI classroom teachers, or have worked extensively in one or more CGI classrooms to learn about CGI in action. One of the best ways for you to gain the required knowledge and experience is to participate fully in a set of CGI workshops and to work intensively in a classroom. If you are not teaching in a classroom at the moment, you should affiliate with a teaching participant and spend as much time as possible learning about CGI in that classroom.

Mutual Respect

Two sets of professionals collaborate in the CGI Professional Development Program: teachers, who have unique knowledge that leaders usually don't have (how to teach in the complex world of classrooms), and workshop leaders, who have unique knowledge that teachers usually don't have (an organized, research-based model that aids in understanding children's thinking and experience with CGI classrooms). The knowledge of teachers and leaders intersect. Certainly most leaders know something about teaching in primary-school classroom and most teachers start with an intuitive knowledge of children's mathematical thinking. Only to the extent that these two sets of professionals respect one another's knowledge can they collaborate in the development of CGI classrooms where children learn with understanding.

Successful leaders respect teachers' knowledge and do not try to dictate how they should teach. We have been most successful when workshops have focused primarily on our specific knowledge (namely, the research-based model of children's thinking and teachers' interpretations of that model) and reflective discussions about using children's thinking to make instructional decisions. This focus is not easy to maintain because teachers have many concerns beyond CGI that are critical and pervade their thinking. However, as much as possible, teachers' other concerns should be addressed in other forums.

Building on Teachers' Knowledge

At the beginning of workshops, teachers often know that some problems are more difficult to solve than others and they are able to generate a variety of solution strategies for many problems. Often, however, this intuitive knowledge is not well organized and does not play a central role in influencing teachers' instruction. As a workshop leader, you need to develop an understanding of teachers' intuitive understandings of children's mathematical thinking in much the same way that teachers develop an understanding of their students' thinking. As teachers are engaged in various activities, you must question, observe, and listen in order to adapt workshop activities to support teacher learning.

Learning Involves Reflection and Communication

Workshop activities should include time for reflecting on the material being covered and on the way that material can be used in teaching. This reflection can be encouraged in a variety of ways: in large- or small-group discussion, by reading CGI materials during workshops, in discussions with other teachers during intervals between workshops. Often reflection is encouraged when teachers are asked to respond to specific questions. The videotapes that accompany this Guide can provide many opportunities for reflection. (See page ii for information on ordering the videotapes.)

Beliefs About Teaching and Learning Mathematics

Although beliefs are not something we usually address directly in our workshops, many of the discussions and activities suggested here do give teachers an opportunity to examine their beliefs. For example, when teachers see a kindergarten child solving a division problem and learn that most kindergartners in CGI classes can solve this problem, their beliefs about children's capabilities may be challenged. We find that teachers' beliefs about learning and teaching mathematics often change as they interact with their students. However, it has not been our experience that teachers' beliefs *must* change before they will change their instruction. Sometimes instruction changes first and changes in beliefs follow later. As with all growth, change in beliefs takes time. We have been most successful when beliefs are discussed in the context of knowledge about children's thinking or instruction.

SUGGESTED ORGANIZATION OF A CGI PROFESSIONAL DEVELOPMENT PROGRAM

Who Should Participate

Throughout this Guide we have referred to those learning about CGI as "participants" rather than teachers. We have found that the Professional Development Program is more successful when principals, mathematics supervisors, special education teachers, and educational assistants as well as classroom teachers learn about CGI. Our experience suggests that although primary-grade teachers are the majority in any workshop, when others learn about the ideas they can provide support to teachers and implement CGI ideas themselves, as appropriate.

Working with Children in Classrooms

Very little about CGI can be understood without interacting with children. Our research suggests that participants develop their understanding of problem types and solution strategies as they interact with children. Usually, each workshop session is followed by specific assignments that have to be completed with children. For example, you can ask teachers to select children with certain characteristics, have the children solve certain problems, record children's solution strategies, and interpret those responses in relation to material covered in the workshop.

All CGI workshops should be organized so that participants can interview either their own students or other children several times. In preparing for the interviews, participants think about problems to be used and questions to be asked. They should have the opportunity to analyze the problems and questions used by the interviewers in the accompanying videotapes and to discuss with peers appropriate problems and questions. You can provide five or six problems or have the teachers (individually or in groups) write problems and identify questions that might be used.

During an interview, the teacher asks a child to solve each problem, finds out how the problem was solved, and records what the child did. Subsequently, the teacher decides what strategy was used and the child's developmental level. Sometimes, pairs of teachers interview individual children. One member of the pair can be responsible for asking questions while the other records what the child does. The two can switch roles halfway through the interview. Together, the pair can then decide what each child knows.

Participants often report that it is difficult to start an interview with a predetermined set of questions. They report that they ask problems that they later realize are too hard or easy for the child, and that, after the interview, many questions remain about a given child's thinking. At that point, teachers generally talk about ways to adapt questions during an interview based on how the child solves the problems.

Time Required to Become a CGI Teacher

It typically takes forty to fifty workshop hours for teachers to develop an initial understanding of children's thinking. These workshop hours can be organized in a variety of ways to accommodate the schedules of leaders, participants, and school systems. Sometimes the workshops are held about once a week for three hours each; sometimes the workshops are scheduled over several weekends. Workshops have also been scheduled during the summer vacation, with follow-up workshops during the school year after teachers have begun to use CGI in classrooms.

After completing the workshop, it takes several years for teachers to become expert in CGI, and teachers need support during those years if they are to become effective CGI teachers. It is essential that you develop a plan for classroom support that can be implemented over a long period. Support might involve common weekly planning time and time to visit each other's classes, or more formal meetings with the original group of teachers from the workshops. Other kinds of support, unique to each community, are also possible. Ideally, teachers will also receive support from their peers. It is ideal if there are at least three or four teachers and an administrator from the same school participating in the workshop.

MATERIALS

Using This Guide

This Guide does not provide prescriptions for how to design a professional development program or lead workshops. Instead, we provide reflections from experienced CGI workshop leaders about their work. We identify what we believe are the major ideas and provide activities that can help teachers learn the major concepts. The Guide concludes with several Appendixes of resources that may be helpful as you design your own workshops. Specifically, Appendix A contains sample workshop agendas; Appendix B included worksheets referred to throughout the guide; Appendix C presents answers to frequently asked questions; and Appendix D contains an annotated bibliography for additional readings.

The reflection chapters are organized according to the chapters in the readings for workshop participants. Each reflection chapter emphasizes major ideas and includes illustrative activities for workshops that have been culled from experienced leaders to assist novice workshop leaders in getting started. Though illustrative activities are included, they do not describe a complete workshop session. You must develop your own activities, depending on your strengths and knowledge and on the knowledge and current understanding of your participants. We do not tell teachers what to do to implement CGI. Neither do we tell workshop leaders what to do. Instead, we try to provide useful knowledge embedded in our general philosophy about how teaching and learning occurs in classrooms and in professional development programs.

Despite the necessity of adaptation, we also believe that the emphasis must continually be on developing an understanding of children's thinking in relation to the CGI research-based framework. As stated previously, teachers have many concerns that cannot be addressed in CGI workshops. Our most successful leaders have been those who maintain a focus on children's thinking.

Readings for Workshop Participants

The accompanying book of readings for workshop participants (*Children's Mathematics: Cognitively Guided Instruction*) is composed of eight chapters:

Chapter 1: Children's Mathematical Thinking
Chapter 2: Addition and Subtraction: Problem Types
Chapter 3: Addition and Subtraction: Children's Solution Strategies
Chapter 4: Multiplication and Division: Problem Types and Children's Solution Strategies
Chapter 5: Problem Solving as Modeling
Chapter 6: Multidigit Number Concepts
Chapter 7: Beginning to Use Cognitively Guided Instruction
Chapter 8: CGI Classrooms

Chapters 1–6 present the research-based framework of children's thinking. Chapters 7 and 8 discuss basic instructional issues in CGI classrooms. All of these chapters should be read and reread during the course of the Professional Development Program. Expert leaders have found that providing workshop time for individuals to read and reflect upon the readings is profitable. The research basis for the CGI approach is presented in an Appendix.

The Videotapes

There are three sets of videotapes. The first set (Videotape I) provides an overview of CGI that can be used with administrators, parents, and teachers as appropriate. The second set (Videotapes II, III, and IV) was developed explicitly to help in teaching and learning about problem types and strategies. Each tape in this set is devoted to one content domain (Videotape II: Addition/Subtraction, Videotape III: Multiplication/Division, Videotape IV: Multidigit Number Concepts). A child is asked to solve a problem, solves it, and, if the strategy used is not readily apparent, explains what s/he did. The logs for these three videotapes identify each episode by number; identify each child by name, grade, and salient characteristics (for example, girl with glasses and white shirt); list the problem; and identify the strategy used. The children shown are solving the problem for the first time and the interviewer is responding as s/he might in a classroom.

The third set of videotapes (Videotapes V–VII) includes edited episodes from ten different CGI classrooms. They were selected to represent novice and expert teachers who organize their classrooms in a variety of ways. Common components of CGI classrooms are seen in each episode: problem solving, children inventing and reporting a variety of solution strategies, and teachers listening and questioning the children about their thinking. In most cases, the episode is followed by an interview with the teacher, which explores why s/he is doing what s/he does.

Excerpts from these videos are contained in the two CD-ROMs that are included with the book of readings for workshop participants. The complete set of videotapes and logs is distributed separately and can be purchased using the contact information provided on the copyright page of this Guide.

Abbreviations of Problem Types

Throughout this Guide we have often used abbreviations of the names of problem types. Those abbreviations are listed below.

JRU	Join (Result Unknown)
JCU	Join (Change Unknown)
JSU	Join (Start Unknown)
SRU	Separate (Result Unknown)
SCU	Separate (Change Unknown)
SSU	Separate (Start Unknown)
PPW-WU	Part-Part-Whole (Whole Unknown)
PPW-PU	Part-Part-Whole (Part Unknown)
CDU	Compare (Difference Unknown)
CQU	Compare (Compare Quantity Unknown)
CRU	Compare (Referent Unknown)
Mult	Multiplication
Mdiv	Measurement Division
Pdiv	Partitive Division

GETTING STARTED

Introducing Cognitively Guided Instruction

The Introduction to the readings for workshop participants emphasizes the importance of understanding in children's learning of mathematics and the necessity of building instruction on what children already know.

BIG IDEAS

The Introduction is participants' first look at some central ideas about children's mathematical thinking. The ideas covered in the Introduction should be emphasized throughout the workshops. These Big Ideas can only be understood by the participants when they are revisited over a long time.

1. Young children have a rich informal knowledge of mathematics that can serve as a basis for developing understanding of mathematics.
2. Mathematics instruction should be based on what children understand about mathematics.
3. When teachers understand a research-based framework of children's thinking, they can make instructional decisions about what and how to teach that expand children's knowledge about mathematics.

Characteristics of CGI classrooms that might be discussed are:

- In CGI classrooms, children spend most of their time solving problems.
- Although CGI teachers do not show children how to solve problems, teachers actively make decisions about mathematics instruction.
- CGI teachers believe that children can figure out how to solve problems without instruction and that solving many problems enables children to grow in their own understanding of mathematics.

ACTIVITIES

Introducing CGI (About Two Hours)

Materials: Videotape I

Many workshop participants have had an introduction to CGI before they attend formal workshops. They may have heard about it at a conference, read an article, or been introduced to it by another teacher. Many of the Big Ideas in this chapter are also covered in the introductory videotape (Videotape I), which can be used to teach the chapter ideas and which often provokes thoughtful discussion about CGI and mathematics teaching. You can have teachers watch this videotape and ask them to answer the question, "What is CGI?" either in individual writing sessions or in small groups. The whole group can then discuss their responses to this question.

Becoming Aware of One's Beliefs (About One Hour)

Participants sometimes can be made aware of their own beliefs as they talk about the beliefs expressed in the Introduction. Working in small groups, participants can be asked to describe a typical math lesson in their classes. Alternatively, they can be asked to finish an open sentence like "*My students learn a lot in math when I . . .*" Many will describe showing children how to do some mathematics. Discussion of the difference between showing children and helping children to build on their existing knowledge could ensue. You should be careful not to be judgmental at this point but rather help participants perceive that different beliefs are possible.

ASSIGNMENTS

Read the Introduction to *Children's Mathematics*.

REFLECTIONS ON TEACHING CHAPTER 1

"Children's Mathematical Thinking"

Chapter 1 in the readings for workshop participants introduces the research-based framework by presenting information about solution strategies and their natural (untaught) use by children. Even though Chapter 1 is very short, the ideas are critical. They are difficult to understand thoroughly and should be revisited many times during the workshop.

BIG IDEAS

1. Young children can solve many mathematical problems that involve addition, subtraction, multiplication, or division (without being shown how to solve them) by directly modeling the action or relationships in the problem.
2. The structure of a problem determines how difficult it is for children to solve and determines their initial solution strategies.

ACTIVITIES

Ranking Problems (About Three Hours)

Materials: Videotape II; Counters; Appendix B: "Rachel's Problems"; Videotape V

This activity works well when teachers work in small groups and typically is done before participants have read Chapters 1 or 2. Participants are given a list of the problems solved by the first child on Videotape II (Rachel) and are asked to rank the problems by considering how hard they would be for children to solve. Discussion of their rankings follows. Participants often recognize that some problems are more difficult than others, but their explanations of why certain problems are difficult tend to be vague. For example, they may say that a Start Unknown problem is difficult because "It is so wordy," or "It is worded in a confusing way."

The videotape of Rachel Directly Modeling the problems on the sheet is viewed (Videotape II @ 1:00–14:21). Stop the tape after each problem so participants can discuss what Rachel does. At the third problem, a Join (Change Unknown) problem, participants can be asked to decide whether the child sees it as subtraction (which is how adults might solve it). The fact that Rachel uses a joining action rather than a subtracting action should be elicited and emphasized.

After participants have watched Rachel solve three or four problems and discussed solutions, they are asked to rerank the problems, taking into consideration how Rachel would solve each remaining problem, and what makes the problems easy or difficult for Rachel. The videotape of Rachel solving the remaining problems can be shown after the solutions and rankings have been discussed. Sometimes participants make lists of their thinking the first time they ranked the problems and then compare this list with their thinking the second time.

Next, participants can be asked to Directly Model a problem such as the one below and compare its difficulty to that of the other problems.

Kevin has 5 bags of cookies with 3 cookies in each bag. He eats 4 cookies. How many cookies does he have left?

The Yttri classroom (Videotape V @ 7:48) provides examples of kindergarten children directly modeling in a classroom situation. You can use this video segment to show Direct Modeling in the classroom.

Solving a Nonstandard Problem (About One and a Half Hours)

Materials: Counters; Videotape V

This activity also focuses on Direct Modeling. Some leaders use it after the participants recognize and have some understanding of Direct Modeling. Others use it to introduce Direct Modeling.

Participants are asked to solve the following problem:

Lizzie collects lizards and beetles. She has 8 creatures in her collection so far. All together they have 36 legs. How many of each kind of creature does she have in her collection?

Participants are encouraged to use whatever strategy makes sense to them, to work in pairs, and to find a second solution strategy after they solve it once. Participants share their solutions, explain why they chose their strategies, discuss how each strategy fits or doesn't fit the structure of the problem, and relate Direct Modeling to the strategies that they have used.

Participants can then view second graders solving the same problem (Videotape V @ 36:09). They discuss what they have seen, focusing the discussion on Direct Modeling by addressing questions such as: "How did the problem structure influence how you solved the problem?" "How did the problem influence how children solved the problem?" or "How did Ms. Kolan use what she understood about Direct Modeling when she interacted with children on this problem?"

ASSIGNMENTS

1. Read Chapter 1 in *Children's Mathematics.*
2. Select four children (in your own classroom if possible). Have those children solve the same problems that Rachel did. (For older children who might have already learned number facts, have them solve Partitive and Measurement Division problems.) Ask them to tell you how the problems were solved, record their strategies, and write two to three sentences about how each child's solutions relates to Direct Modeling.
3. Have children solve some nonroutine problems and be prepared to report how the problems were solved and to discuss the solutions in relation to Direct Modeling. The following nonroutine problems have been used successfully:

19 children are going to the zoo in a minibus. The minibus has 7 seats. How many children will have to sit 3 to a seat and how many will have to sit 2 to a seat?

Maggie has 3 boxes of cupcakes with 4 cupcakes in each box. She eats 5 cupcakes. How many does she have left?

In a field with cows and chickens, I counted 30 feet and 11 heads. How many cows were in the field? How many chickens were in the field?

REFLECTIONS ON TEACHING CHAPTER 2

"Addition and Subtraction: Problem Types"

Although addition and subtraction problem types are discussed in Chapter 2 of the readings for workshop participants and children's solution strategies for addition and subtraction are presented in Chapter 3, the major ideas are interdependent. Thus, many workshop activities involve Big Ideas from both of these chapters—it is difficult to understand the Big Ideas of one without understanding the Big Ideas of the other. It is a good idea to briefly introduce the Big Ideas of Chapter 2, to give participants an initial understanding of problem structure, and then move on to children's solution strategies (Chapter 3) as soon as participants demonstrate some initial understanding of the problem types. You may then want to come back to a deeper look at Chapter 2.

BIG IDEAS

1. Stated action and relationships form the *structure* of addition/subtraction word problems and distinguish among them.
2. The *structure* of a problem reflects how children *solve* it.
3. Both the *structure* and *location of the unknown quantity* determine the relative difficulty of the different problems.

ACTIVITIES

Building the Classification of Word Problems Chart (About Two Hours)

Materials: Videotape II; Counters

We present this activity as a vignette to illustrate how some leaders work with participants. You will have to modify the example to fit your particular circumstances. Only portions of the activity are presented because of space considerations.

The specific purpose of this activity is to provide participants with an initial understanding of the Classification of Word Problems chart (see Figure 1 on the following page) by constructing it themselves. In the vignette, an experienced CGI leader uses a combination of discussion, directed questioning, videotape viewing, and summarizing to emphasize that the problem type categorization matches children's thinking about addition and subtraction. The problems used (shown below) match those solved by Rachel (Videotape II @ 1:00–3:33). These problems may have been used earlier in the workshop, but our experience indicates they can be used again.

1. *Lucy has 8 fish. She wants to buy 5 more fish. How many fish would Lucy have then?* (JRU)
2. *TJ had 13 chocolate chip cookies. At lunch she ate 5 of these cookies. How many cookies did TJ have left?* (SRU)

Problem Type			
Join	*(Result Unknown)* Connie had 5 marbles. Juan gave her 8 more marbles. How many marbles does Connie have altogether?	*(Change Unknown)* Connie has 5 marbles. How many marbles does she need to have 13 marbles altogether?	*(Start Unknown)* Connie had some marbles. Juan gave her 5 more marbles. Now she has 13 marbles. How many marbles did Connie have to start with?
Separate	*(Result Unknown)* Connie had 13 marbles. She gave 5 to Juan. How many marbles does Connie have left?	*(Change Unknown)* Connie had 13 marbles. She gave some to Juan. Now she has 5 marbles left. How many marbles did Connie give to Juan?	*(Start Unknown)* Connie had some marbles. She gave 5 to Juan. Now she has 8 marbles left. How many marbles did Connie have to start with?
Part-Part-Whole	*(Whole Unknown)* Connie has 5 red marbles and 8 blue marbles. How many marbles does she have?		*(Part Unknown)* Connie has 13 marbles. 5 are red and the rest are blue. How many blue marbles does Connie have?
Compare	*(Difference Unknown)* Connie has 13 marbles. Juan has 5 marbles. How many more marbles does Connie have than Juan?	*(Compare Quantity Unknown)* Juan has 5 marbles. Connie has 8 more than Juan. How many marbles does Connie have?	*(Referent Unknown)* Connie has 13 marbles. She has 5 more marbles than Juan. How many marbles does Juan have?

FIGURE 1 *Classification of Word Problems*

3. *Janelle has 7 trolls in her collection. How many more does she have to buy to have 11 trolls?* (JCU)

The first three problems are discussed by the Leader (L) and Participants (P) before the participants view Rachel solving them.

L: Which two of these problems are most alike and why?
P: Problems 2 and 3 are alike because they are subtraction problems.
P: Problem 3 is harder because it has the key word "more" in it, but if you add 7 and 11 together you will not get the right answer.
P: Problem 3 would be harder for my students than the others.
L: Is there anything about how these problems would be directly modeled that might make problem 3 harder than problems 1 or 2?
[Discussion follows]
L: As we watch a first-grade child solve these problems, think about how they are alike and different for the child solving them. Do they differ in difficulty, and if so, why?

General discussion followed the viewing of the videotape of Rachel solving the first three problems. The leader had participants focus on whether Rachel did joining or separating actions to solve the problems. Problems 1 and 3 involve joining whereas Problem 2 involves separating. Even though many teachers solved Problem 3 by subtracting, Rachel solved it using a joining action. Teachers were asked to write one problem with a joining action and one with a separating action. They then shared their problems and discussed them.

> *L*: Was Problem 3 more difficult for Rachel to solve than the other problems?
> *P*: Yes, because it just wasn't as straightforward as Problem 1 or 2. The child just can't go step by step through the problem and do what it says.
> *L*: Think about being able to go step by step through a problem as we watch Rachel solve [the next problem on the videotape].

Max had some money. He spent $9.00 on a video game. Now he has $7.00 left. How much money did Max have to start with? (SSU; Videotape II @ 3:34)

After much discussion, participants decide that the problem probably can't be solved step by step and that it is harder than Problem 3 because Rachel didn't know where to start.

> *L*: We have said that problems can vary with respect to the type of action in them which we have called joining or separating. Problems can also vary with respect to where the unknown occurs in the story. In Problem 4 you are looking for the starting quantity so the start is unknown. Where is the unknown in Problem 3?
> *P*: In the middle.
> *L*: When the unknown is in the middle, we call the problem a *Change Unknown* problem. Where are the unknowns in Problems 1 and 2?
> [Discussion follows]
> *L*: [After putting the chart shown in Figure 2 on the overhead projector] Either a joining [top row] or a separating [second row] action can be embedded in addition and subtraction problems. There are three different places where these Joining and Separating problems can have

1. Lucy has 8 fish. She wants to buy 5 more fish. How many fish would Lucy have then?	3. Janelle has 7 trolls in her collection. How many more does she have to buy to have 11 trolls?	
2. TJ had 13 chocolate chip cookies. At lunch she ate 5 of those cookies. How many cookies did TJ have left?		4. Max had some money. He spent $9.00 on a video game. Now he has $7.00 left. How much money did Max have to start with?

FIGURE 2
Leader's Problem Type Chart Used to Distinguish Unknown Quantities

unknown quantities: Result—Problems 1 and 2, Change—Problem 3, or Start—Problem 4.

The leader then labeled each problem type using the CGI names and asked the teachers to work in pairs to compose a Join (Change Unknown) problem and a Separate (Result Unknown) problem (the types shown on the chart). When teachers were finished, the group listened to each other's problems to decide what problem types they were.

The leader then showed the group the following problem:

> *11 children were playing in the sandbox. Some children went home. There were 3 children still playing in the sandbox. How many children went home? (SCU)*

After consensus was reached that it was a Separate (Change Unknown) problem, participants were asked to write a problem that would fit the top right corner of the chart, a Join (Start Unknown) problem. Problems were shared, and their placements discussed. Throughout the discussion, the leader focused on the *action* and the *location of the unknown* in each problem.

Learning About No-Action Problems: Part-Part-Whole and Compare

A new idea emerged when the following Part-Part-Whole (Part Unknown) problem had been written and shared by a participant who mistakenly thought it was a Separate (Result Unknown):

> *There were some robins and 13 cardinals in the tree. There were 19 birds in the tree. How many robins were in the tree?*

The leader asked if everyone thought it was a Separate (Result Unknown) problem. Most participants agreed that it was. Participants were then asked to think about the time sequence in the problem (what happened first, what changed, and what resulted). Time sequences usually indicate action. When a time sequence could not be identified, the leader commented that problems with no time sequence do not have action and thus cannot be Separate problems. The leader said that this problem is a Part-Part-Whole problem. (Typically, many participants have trouble seeing that some problems have no action and that there was no action in this problem. In these problems, a situation is described, but there is no story that occurs over time. This is an idea that will need to be returned to many times.)

Participants were asked to Directly Model the next problem on the videotape (Videotape II @ 4:41):

> *Willy has 12 crayons. Lucy has 7 crayons. How many more crayons does Willy have than Lucy? (CDU)*

They then used that experience to help them think about whether or not the problem had action.

If a participant used a Separating From or a Joining To strategy (and several did), the leader asked them what it was about the problem that told them to separate the sets or to join something. She used questions such as "Where were Lucy's crayons and Willie's crayons?" The leader emphasized that in Direct Modeling all quantities and the action or situation of the problem are represented.

The leader summarized by saying, "In addition to classifying problems by the type of action and location of unknown, you can classify problems according to whether or not they *have* action. There are two different types of problems that have no action. Those like Problem 6 (the crayons problem), which describe comparison situations, are called Compare problems." She then gave examples of the three types of Compare problems. Discussion followed about the two types of Part-Part-Whole problems, and how they differed from the Join, Separate, and Compare problems. Among the points raised was that there is no time sequence (nothing changes over time).

In order to summarize the points they had raised, the complete Classification of Word Problems chart (Figure 1) was shown and discussed. Emphasized was Action/No Action, Joining/Separating/Part-Part-Whole/Comparing, and the location of the unknown.

The leader ended the session by saying:

> The problem type chart is a powerful tool for understanding how children think about addition/subtraction problems in planning further instruction. During the workshop and in your classroom you can refer to this chart as you need help in classifying problems. Typically teachers learn to classify problems without the aid of the chart after they use these problems with their children and come to understand how their children think. We will continually review these problems as we work together.

OTHER ACTIVITIES TO LEARN THE PROBLEM TYPES

All of the following activities assume that teachers have some knowledge of the Classification of Word Problems chart. These activities are interspersed throughout a workshop and typically are done after the activity described above. These activities can also be used or reused as review at a later time.

Writing a Set of Problems (About Two Hours)

Materials: Appendix B: "Blank Problem Type Chart"

Blank problem type charts (see Appendix B) are provided, and participants write a set of problems around a theme that they plan to use with children. Because children often surprise adults with what they can do, participants are encouraged to either choose numbers a little higher than what they anticipate their students can use, or be prepared to change the numbers as appropriate. As the problems are reviewed, information about the teachers' understanding of the problem types can be gained and feedback can be given.

Identifying a Set of Problems (Less Than One Hour)

Materials: Appendix B: "Problems to Be Identified: Sample Set"

Participants are given a set of problems (Appendix B: "Problems to Be Identified: Sample Set") and asked to identify where the problem fits in the problem type chart. Problems that don't exactly fit the problem wording on the chart are included in order to encourage teachers to look beyond surface characteristics. Problems with nonsequential order are also included. For example, the first problem in the following set is more difficult to classify than the second, yet both are Separate (Change Unknown) problems.

> *When I left the store I counted my money and found I had 29 dollars. Before I went into the store I had 81 dollars. How much money did I spend at the store?*
>
> *I went to the store with 81 dollars. I spent some money, and now I have 29 dollars. How much money did I spend?*

Extraneous information also makes problems more difficult to classify. For example the first problem in the following set is more difficult to classify than the second.

Carlos and Peggy want to save money for a puppy. They got some money for raking leaves. They counted it, and they had 6 dollars. It still wasn't enough money for a puppy. They had only 10 more days to save enough money to buy that puppy. They needed to have 15 dollars all together. How much money did they still need to earn?

Carlos and Peggy have 6 dollars. They need 15 dollars to buy a puppy. How much more money do they need?

Problems are also harder to classify when they include unrelated action in a nonaction problem. For example, the first problem below is more difficult to classify than the second, yet they are both Part-Part-Whole (Whole Unknown) problems.

Andy and Alec went to pick apples. Andy picked 8 apples. Alec picked 7 apples. How many apples did they pick?

Andy and Alec have a basket of apples. There are 8 red and 7 green apples in the basket. How many apples are in the basket?

Finding Someone Else with Your Problem Type (Forty-Five Minutes)

Materials: Index Cards with Story Problems on Them

Problem types can be reviewed by giving each teacher a story problem and having them find another person who has a problem of the same type. In this activity, participants have to talk with each other about various problems in order to identify a common problem type.

ASSIGNMENTS

1. Read Chapter 2 in *Children's Mathematics.*
2. Try problems with children and be prepared to report at the next workshop about children's solution strategies.
3. Write one of each of the eleven problem types. Have someone check that your problems are correctly categorized. Make a copy of your problems for each workshop participant.

REFLECTIONS ON TEACHING CHAPTER 3

"Addition and Subtraction: Children's Solution Strategies"

Chapter 3 in the readings for workshop participants is about the strategies typically used by young children to solve addition and subtraction problems: Direct Modeling, Counting, Derived Facts, and Recall of Number Facts. Children's use of the various strategies develops sequentially starting with Direct Modeling, continuing through various Counting strategies, to use of Derived Facts (based on relationships), and finally to Recall of Number Facts.

BIG IDEAS

1. Distinctions among problem types are reflected in children's solution processes.
2. At the most immature level, children use physical objects to directly model the action or relationships in each problem.
3. As children mature, their strategies become more abstract and efficient. *Direct Modeling* strategies are replaced by *Counting* strategies, which in turn are replaced with *Derived Facts* strategies and *Recall of Number Facts*.
4. Strategies at different levels of abstraction are related.

Big Ideas for Direct Modeling

1. Direct Modeling provides a basis for the learning of the other strategies.
2. Direct Modeling is not the same as using counters to solve problems. Children can Directly Model without using counters and can use counters without Directly Modeling.
3. In order for a strategy to be considered Direct Modeling, the action or situation of the *strategy* has to match the action or situation of the *problem*, and all quantities in the problem must be represented. A common misconception is that any strategy in which all sets in a problem are represented is a Direct Modeling strategy. For example, teachers often call a Joining All strategy used to solve a Separate (Start Unknown) problem Direct Modeling.
4. Some problems are more difficult to Directly Model than others. For example, Join (Change Unknown) problems are more difficult to model than Join or Separate (Result Unknown) problems.

Big Ideas for Other Strategies

1. The use of fingers does not determine whether or not a child is using a Counting strategy. Children can use their fingers and not be using Counting strategies, and children can use Counting strategies without using their fingers.

2. There are Counting strategies that directly match the action in the problem for many of the problem types, whereas for other problems there is no related Counting strategy.
3. Children will first use Counting strategies that match the action of a problem and will eventually become flexible and use Counting strategies that don't exactly match the actions of problems.
4. Certain problem types and number combinations encourage the use of Counting strategies and are good to use to assess use of Counting strategies.
5. Children know and use *some* facts to solve problems starting at a very young age.
6. Children rely on efficient Counting and Derived Facts strategies (even when they use them covertly) for a long time before they rely on Recall of Number Facts to solve problems.

Big Ideas for Relationships Among Strategies

1. There are important relationships among strategies that are seen when a child is at a certain level of development. For example, there is a relationship between the Direct Modeling strategy for a problem and the Counting strategy a child is likely to use to solve that problem. Put another way, Counting strategies can be described as abstractions of Direct Modeling strategies.
2. Children in any class will be at different levels of understanding and will use different strategies to solve the same problems.
3. Children naturally progress through the levels without direct instruction.
4. Understanding children's solution strategies involves a complex set of ideas. Many participants come to understand problem types (Chapter 2) long before they understand children's solution strategies (Chapter 3). Solution strategies and their relation to problem types and each other is a theme that permeates the entire Professional Development Program.

ACTIVITIES

Using Videotape II to Learn Solution Strategies (About Three Hours, Usually in One-Hour Segments)

Materials: Videotape II

Many workshop leaders initiate discussion of solution strategies by using selected episodes of Videotape II, "Children's Strategies for Addition/Subtraction." A typical way to use the tape is to select one episode and stop the tape after the problem is read. Leaders then ask participants to identify the problem type and describe a specific strategy for solving the problem (e.g., "How would you use a Counting strategy to solve this problem?"). The episode is then viewed and discussed.

Participants can also watch the videotapes individually or in small groups. To help them reflect on what they are seeing, they can fill in a sheet that lists the problems (derived from the Videotape Logs) and leaves blanks for identifying the problem type, the strategy type, and the specific strategy. It is also useful to listen to the problem type, watch the child solve the problem, and then ask participants to describe and classify the strategy used.

The following episodes on Videotape II are useful for certain ideas. (The episodes are identified by number in the Logs.)

- Direct Modeling without counters: Episodes 18, 21, and 25
- Separating To vs. Separating From: Episode 28 vs. Episode 21

- Direct Modeling a Start Unknown problem: Episode 29
- Children's strategies that do not match the problems' structures: Episodes 30–33

Describing Strategies for Particular Problems (About One and a Half Hours)

Materials: Appendix B: "How Would Children Solve These Problems?"; Counters

Participants are given a list of problems. In small groups they describe Direct Modeling, Counting, and Facts strategies that go with each problem. Participants are asked to work each strategy as a child would. A supplement to this activity is to ask participants to identify other strategies children might be likely to use to solve each problem.

Finding a Problem for a Strategy (About One and a Half Hours)

Materials: Appendix B: "Finding a Problem for a Strategy"

Participants are given a description of a specific strategy, asked to write a problem that matches the strategy, and then asked to identify the problem type. For example:

> Janet draws seven lines as she counts: "1, 2, 3, 4, 5, 6, 7." She then leaves a space and draws six more lines as she counts: "8, 9, . . . 13." She looks at her drawing and counts the second set of lines: "1, 2, 3, 4, 5, 6." She says her answer is, "6."

Participants can figure out that Janet employed a Direct Modeling strategy in solving this Join (Change Unknown) problem. They can then write a specific problem that fits the strategy she used.

Learning About the Development Levels (Time Varies)

The Children's Solutions Strategies Chart 1 appears in Chapter 3 of the readings for workshop participants (Figure 3.7 on page 30 of *Children's Mathematics*) and is a synthesis of the levels of development that children go through as they become mature problem solvers. (A copy of this chart also appears in Appendix B of this Guide.) You will need to discuss this chart with participants.

Role-Playing (About Two Hours)

Materials: Index Cards (See Below for Preparation Instructions); Counters

A group of four participants role-plays mock interviews. Each group is given a set of index cards, each of which includes a description of a child's thinking (see below). You will need to prepare these cards before teaching this activity. Two people assume the role of the interviewer and two assume the role of a child with the described characteristics. The people who are to act the child are to respond to the interviewers' questions in a manner consistent with the description of that child's level of understanding. The people who take the role of the interviewer are to find out as much as possible about the child's mathematical understanding by posing problems and asking questions. Specifically they are to ask "the child" a series of story problems to find out how s/he thinks about mathematics. (It typically takes between four and seven problems to fully describe a child.) Once a round has been completed, participants in each group change roles and get a new description of a child.

The descriptions given to the teams are mixed so that they do not progress from least to most sophisticated. This can be a difficult activity for participants. To play either role, participants need a good understanding of problem types, solution strategies, and the levels of development. Sometimes the leader demonstrates playing each part with a partner before asking participants to do the activity. After the teams have done several role-plays, a whole-group discussion ensues. In this discussion, the focus is on the relationships among the strategies and problem types, which can be elicited by asking questions such as "What problem type would you ask to see if a child could Count On?" or "Which problems gave you a lot of information and why?"

The following descriptions of children have been used successfully in this activity:

- Direct Modeler who cannot plan ahead
- Direct Modeler who can plan ahead
- Direct Modeler who can plan ahead, sometimes uses facts, and knows many doubles
- Direct Modeler who can plan ahead, will Count On with Join (Result Unknown) problems if the number to be added is small
- Counter who does not know to Count On from larger
- Counter who does not know to Count On from larger, will sometimes use Facts, especially facts based on tens
- Counter who will Count On from larger and has trouble Counting Back, but will try
- Counter who will Count On from larger and can Count Back
- Child who has flexible choice of strategies but will most often use Counting strategies
- Child who has flexible choice of strategies but most often uses both Derived Facts and Recall of Number Facts

ASSIGNMENTS

1. Interview a set of children and bring reports of their solution strategies to the next workshop.
2. Read Chapter 3 in *Children's Mathematics*.
3. Write a set of problems, interview three children, record how each solved the problems.

REFLECTIONS ON TEACHING CHAPTER 4

"Multiplication and Division: Problem Types and Children's Solution Strategies"

Although multiplication and division problems are included in CGI classrooms almost from the very beginning in the Professional Development Program, the problem types and solution strategies of multiplication and division are usually presented after those of addition and subtraction. Because the ideas about addition and subtraction complement those of multiplication and division, it is not necessary to understand one completely before the other is introduced. Many of the major concepts of addition and subtraction can be reviewed and revisited in the context of multiplication and division. In addition to the activities described below, many of the activities described in previous chapters for learning about addition and subtraction can be modified to address multiplication and division.

BIG IDEAS

1. Multiplication/division problems are appropriate for beginning problem solvers.
2. The analysis of addition/subtraction problems and the solution strategies used by children can be extended to multiplication/division.
3. Multiplication/division problems commonly used in the primary grades involve three quantities to be combined or partitioned.[1]
4. The progression of use of various strategies for solving multiplication/division problems is similar to that seen with addition/subtraction: Direct Modeling, Counting, Derived Facts, Recall of Number Facts.
5. Children deal with remainders by considering the context of the problem.
6. Understanding multiplication/division problem types and solution strategies is the basis for understanding our base-ten number system.

ACTIVITIES

Many activities described for addition and subtraction in earlier chapters of this Guide can be modified and used for multiplication and division. (Specifically, in "Reflections on Teaching Chapter 2" see Building the Classification of Word Problems Chart, Writing a Set of Problems, Identifying a Set of Problems, Finding Someone Else with Your Problem Type. In "Reflections on Teaching Chapter 3," see

1. Chapter 4 in the readings for workshop participants includes an enriched discussion of other multiplication/division problem types: Rate, Multiplicative Comparison, Area and Array, and Combination. Typically these are addressed briefly, if at all, in an introductory workshop. Multiplication/division can be taught adequately in the primary grades even if teachers do not understand these more advanced ideas. Whether or not to include them in the Professional Development Program is left to your discretion.

Using Videotape II to Learn Solution Strategies, Describing Strategies for Particular Problems, Finding a Problem for a Strategy, Learning About the Development Levels, and Role-Playing.)

Introducing the Multiplication/Division Problem Types Using Direct Modeling (About One Hour)

Materials: Index Cards (See Preparation Instructions Below); Counters

Give teachers a diverse set of multiplication and division problems on index cards (one problem per card) and ask them to sort the problems so those that would be Directly Modeled in a similar way are together.

For example, the following set includes all three types of problems, and some of the problems have remainders. (You could use these problems on your index cards.)

> *Chih had 5 bags of candy with 7 pieces of candy in each bag. How many pieces of candy did Chih have?*
>
> *At Sally's birthday party there were 15 children and 3 blankets. If the same number of children sat on each blanket, how many children sat on each blanket?*
>
> *Brenda raises puppies. Each mother dog had 4 puppies. She has 3 mother dogs. How many puppies were there?*
>
> *Maria has 17 fish. If 3 fish can be put into one fish bowl, how many bowls does she need to hold her fish?*
>
> *Lee collects stamps. He has 45 stamps. If he sticks 9 stamps on each page, how many pages would he fill with stamps?*
>
> *Mr. Wong has 4 children. He wants his children to share 12 marbles so that they each get the same amount. How many marbles should Mr. Wong give each child?*
>
> *19 children are going to the circus. 5 children can ride in each car. How many cars are needed so that all the children can go to the circus?*

Participants who do not understand how to classify these problems need more time discussing Direct Modeling. When participants have classified the problems into three groups, label each group according to its formal name and offer a definition for each problem type. Concurrently, remainders and their relationship to the context of the problem can be discussed.

Using Videotape III and Classroom Tapes to Learn Solution Strategies (About Two Hours for the Entire Activity)

Materials: Videotapes III and IV

The following episodes on Videotape III are useful for certain ideas specific to multiplication and division. (The episodes are identified by number in the Logs.)

- Interchanging the numbers that represent the number of sets and the number in each set: Episodes 8 and 10; Meyer classroom (Videotape VII @ 21:21)
- The variations of Direct Modeling strategies for Partitive and Measurement Division problems; Partitive Division: Episodes 3 and 4; Measurement Division: Episodes 2 and 15

- Measurement Division encourages the use of Counting strategies more so than does Partitive Division: Episodes 7, 8, and 19

Creating Problems with Remainders (About One Hour)

Materials: Counters

Participants are given a number sentence such as 46 ÷ 4 and asked to write and share as many corresponding word problems as they can. They are asked specifically to find problems with the answers 11, 12, 11 1/2, and 2. (See Chapter 4, p. 43, in *Children's Mathematics*, "What to Do with What's Left Over.")

ASSIGNMENTS

1. Read Chapter 4 in *Children's Mathematics*.
2. Use multiplication/division problems in your classes. (Participants can be organized into same-grade-level groups and given time to plan how they would do this. They could write multiplication/division problems around a theme that all could use in their classes, or decide to include a few multiplication/division problems in their next addition/subtraction lesson.) Although you may have already tried CGI ideas in an ongoing class, implement CGI with multiplication/division problems to find out about children's thinking and to begin to get a feel for how CGI works in classrooms. As you try the problems in classes, select a few children to focus on in order to find out how they solve problems. Record their solutions and share them with the colleagues in your grade-level groups.

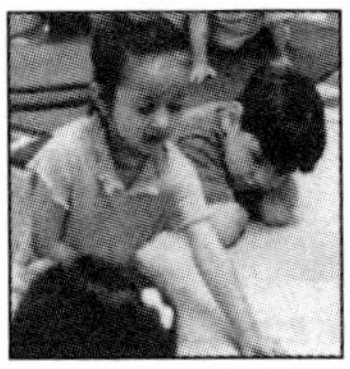

REFLECTIONS ON TEACHING CHAPTER 5

"Problem Solving as Modeling"

This chapter presents the unifying theme of the research-based model of children's thinking: Children naturally attempt to model the action or relationships presented by the contexts of a variety of addition/subtraction and multiplication/division word problems. Since Counting strategies are abstractions of Modeling strategies, it is helpful to think of children's early solution strategies as ways to model problems rather than as a collection of distinct strategies. A primary goal of CGI is to help children build upon and extend these early intuitive modeling skills.

BIG IDEAS

1. Modeling is a unifying theme for understanding children's thinking in addition, subtraction, multiplication, and division.
2. The research-based framework of children's thinking becomes more meaningful and useful when teachers have an understanding of this more general picture.

ACTIVITIES

Judging Relative Difficulty (About One Hour)

Materials: Appendix B: "Addition/Subtraction Relative Difficulty" Worksheet and Responses

Participants are given pairs of problems and asked to decide which problem is the more difficult one and why. (See the "Relative Difficulty" worksheets.) After working through a set of problems, conclusions are discussed. There is not necessarily a right answer for each pair. In some pairs, one problem is clearly easier to Direct Model than the other. In others, the more difficult problem is harder to identify.

ASSIGNMENTS

Read Chapter 5 in *Children's Mathematics*.

REFLECTIONS ON TEACHING CHAPTER 6
"Multidigit Number Concepts"

Children's thinking about problem solving with multidigit numbers starts by initially learning that collections of tens (or hundreds or thousands[1]) can be worked with in the same way as single digits—that is, they can be added, subtracted, multiplied, or divided. Using multidigit numbers to solve problems develops in a parallel fashion as problem solving with single-digit numbers. Multiplication and Measurement Division problems help children learn to group by ten. Children should be given experiences with multidigit numbers almost concurrently with single-digit numbers.

BIG IDEAS

1. In order to understand and work with multidigit numbers, children must learn that collections of tens (or hundreds or thousands) can be counted and talked about just like individual units.
2. Learning about groups of ten can be done in the context of Multiplication and Measurement Division problems (discussed in Chapter 4 of *Children's Mathematics*) and by working directly with objects grouped by tens.
3. Without instruction, children can construct meaningful solutions to problems involving grouping by ten.
4. Solution strategies constructed by children to solve multidigit number problems have direct parallels with and are natural extensions of the strategies they construct for single-digit numbers.
5. Children invent algorithms for solving multidigit number problems after they have had many experiences solving problems with single- and multidigit numbers and working with groups of ten. These invented algorithms can be categorized so that they are more easily understood by participants.
6. Children should have many experiences solving problems that involve multidigit numbers even if their understanding of working with groups of ten is limited.
7. Teachers can facilitate children's invention of multidigit algorithms by providing many experiences with grouping by ten, by asking children to solve many problems that involve groups of ten, and by helping children recognize the ease of using tens in solving problems.

1. Groups of one million and larger can be worked with similarly, but for reasons of space and readability, we refer only to tens.

ACTIVITIES

Although teachers come to understand the information in this chapter about as readily as they do that in others, learning how to use it in the classroom appears to be harder for teachers. There are several possible reasons for this. First, whereas teachers find that their students understand more than they expected about problems with small numbers, teachers often find that their students understand less than they expected about base-ten number concepts. Second, because beginning CGI teachers learn quite well how to assess whether a child understands an idea, they often find that their traditional place-value activities are not understood by children and it is somewhat unclear what activities to use to help children come to understand base-ten ideas. A third difficulty is posed by students who have learned rote procedures, such as Standard Algorithms, for solving multidigit problems. These children are often reluctant to stop using these procedures even if they don't understand them.

When working with the concepts in Chapter 6, participants need to return continually to a discussion of choice of numbers in problems. Whereas *problem type* is a major determinant of problem difficulty for the small-number domain, the choice of *number* has a significant influence on problem difficulty for children who are learning to use base-ten concepts to solve problems. Participants need to understand the distinctions among working with decade numbers (those that end with zero), with nondecade numbers, and with problems that do or do not require numbers to be regrouped (changing tens for ones).

Watching Videotapes of Children Solving Problems (About Two Hours)

Materials: Videotape IV; Base-Ten Blocks; Connecting Cubes

Videotape IV can be used in much the same way as Videotapes II and III. In addition, several specific issues are important. One is that children can and should solve problems with large numbers even if their understanding of base-ten is limited. Episodes 1, 4, and 7 on Videotape IV show children who do this. Even though these children have difficulty with counting, they meaningfully engage in solving these problems. Also, these children practice counting as they solve the problems. Children need not and should not be deprived of problem-solving experiences just because their counting skills are not yet well developed.

Another issue illustrated in Videotape IV is children's use of symbols.[2] There are at least three uses illustrated:

- Several children write down the numbers in the problem to help remember them.
- The children in Episodes 10, 14, 15, and 18 write a traditional number sentence and solve the problem by either Modeling or Invented Algorithms. These children use symbols as records of what they have done or what the problem is about. This use of symbols can lead to a discussion about how teachers can help children learn to use informal strategies to solve traditional number sentences.
- The children in Episodes 17, 24, and 31 use symbols to keep track of where they are as they solve problems with Invented Algorithms. Many children understand how to use Invented Algorithms to solve problems but have trouble remembering what steps they have already taken and what their running total is, especially when the numbers are large.

---

2. Children also use symbols to communicate their solution strategies to the teacher, who is not necessarily there when the child solves the problem. See Statz (Videotape VI @ 19:55) and Garden (Videotape VII @ 0:00).

Another issue that can be addressed with this tape is problem difficulty. Although Separating problems are not more difficult than Joining problems for children who Directly Model with Ones, using Invented Algorithms for Separating problems is more difficult than it is for Joining problems. Participants can engage in discussions about this increased difficulty using Episodes 10, 14, 20, 21, and 30.

Role-Playing (About Two Hours)

Materials: Base-Ten Blocks; Connecting Cubes; Index Cards (See Preparation Instructions Below)

The Role-Playing activity (described in "Reflections on Teaching Chapter 3" section of this Guide) can easily be adapted for use in learning multidigit number concepts. The following descriptions of children's understandings can be used:

- Models with Ones, does not use any groupings of ten to solve problems.
- Models to solve problems. Can use tens to make the initial set(s) used to solve the problem. Solves problems by counting sets by ones.
- Uses Counting strategies that do not make use of base-ten concepts. Direct Models with Tens when it is hard to keep track using Counting By Ones strategies.
- Direct Models with Tens. Cannot Direct Model with Tens for Join (Change Unknown) problem.
- Direct Models with Tens for all problems.
- Direct Models with Tens. Can use Invented Algorithms for Join (Result Unknown) problems if no regrouping is involved.
- Uses Invented Algorithms for all Join (Result Unknown) problems. Uses Invented Algorithms for Separate and Join (Change Unknown) problems only when no regrouping is involved. Might try Invented Algorithms for Separate and Join (Change Unknown) problems with regrouping but is unsuccessful.
- Uses Invented Algorithms for all problems.

Judging Relative Difficulty (About One Hour)

Materials: Appendix B: "Multidigit Numbers Relative Difficulty" Worksheets and Responses; Base-Ten Blocks; Connecting Cubes

The Judging Relative Difficulty activity (described in the "Reflections on Teaching Chapter 5" section of this Guide) can also be adapted for use here. One issue addressed in this activity is that the relative difficulty of each problem is related to the type of strategy a child uses to solve it. For example, although it is more difficult to use an Invented Algorithm to solve problem 1B (see "Multidigit Numbers Relative Difficulty" worksheets) than it is to solve problem 1A, these problems are equally difficult to solve by Direct Modeling with Tens or by Direct Modeling with Ones. The story is a little different for the Separating problems in set 6. Although these problems are equally difficult to solve by Modeling with Ones, the problem with regrouping is more difficult to solve both by Direct Modeling with Tens and by using Invented Algorithms. (Similar differences exist with sets 3 and 4.)

Exploring Different Strategies with Different Problem Types (About One and a Half Hours)

Materials: Base-Ten Blocks

One way for teachers to learn about the variety of different multidigit strategies children use is to have them generate strategies. There are many different methods for organizing this—one is described below.

Teachers work in small groups, with the following problems distributed so that each problem is solved by two groups. Each small group generates as many strategies as they can for their problem.

Kevin has 294 baseball cards. He wants to have 723 baseball cards. How many more cards does he need to collect?

The zookeeper gave the elephant 723 peanuts. She ate 294 of them. How many peanuts were left?

The giant pumpkin had 723 pumpkin seeds in it. The medium pumpkin had 294 pumpkin seeds in it. How many more pumpkin seeds were in the giant pumpkin than in the medium one?

After the groups generate strategies for the problem they are given, participants reorganize into new groups, comprised of one member from each of the previous groups and discuss the strategies.

There are two major goals for this activity. One is for participants to see that many different strategies can be used to solve the problem 723 – 294 =. The other is for participants to see that certain problem types encourage certain strategies more than do others.

Writing an Interview to Assess a Child's Understanding of Base-Ten Number Concepts (Between Four and Six Hours)

Because participants often feel overwhelmed with the amount of knowledge related to children's understanding of multidigit numbers, they often ask for a list of benchmarks that children pass through as they advance in their understanding of base-ten concepts. However, although certain understandings are more advanced than others (using Invented Algorithms for Separating versus using Invented Algorithms for Joining problems), there is no single hierarchically arranged list of benchmarks that children pass through.

One method to help participants organize their understandings about base-ten number concepts is to have them write an interview to assess a child's understanding of base-ten. Participants reread Chapter 6 in *Children's Mathematics* and list the important ideas that children need to understand about base-ten. Following this, the entire group compiles one master list. In small groups, with the leader helping as necessary, participants use this master list to write an interview for assessing a child's understanding. Before the next workshop, participants assess several children's knowledge and at the next session share descriptions of what each child understood about base-ten and the effectiveness of the interview. Interviews are then revised based on this discussion.

The purpose of this activity is to help participants organize their understandings of how children think about base-ten number concepts. Although the written interviews are seldom used to assess understandings of all students in a class, they are often referred to in order to help make decisions about what types of problems an individual child needs next, or what types of problems can be given to an entire class.

ASSIGNMENTS

1. Read Chapter 6 in *Children's Mathematics.*
2. Interview three children to assess their understanding of base-ten number concepts. Write a paragraph about each child.

REFLECTIONS ON TEACHING CHAPTER 7

"Beginning to Use Cognitively Guided Instruction"

Even though Chapters 7 and 8 are placed near the end of the readings for workshop participants, most experienced workshop leaders address issues dealing with instruction concurrently with issues dealing with children's thinking. These chapters can be read profitably at almost any point.

Chapter 7 emphasizes the idea that although teaching mathematics the CGI way is fundamentally different from traditional mathematics teaching, getting started is relatively easy. Even though it takes a long time to feel comfortable with CGI, the rewards for both teacher and students are worth the struggle. This chapter can be read soon after participants begin to learn about problem types and solution strategies. One of the goals of this chapter is to encourage teachers to start giving problems to children (and having them report their solution strategies) before the teachers have learned or feel they have mastered the entire research-based framework of children's thinking.

BIG IDEAS

1. Because teaching mathematics the CGI way is fundamentally different from traditional methods of teaching mathematics, learning to be a CGI teacher can take a long time.
2. Getting started with CGI is easy. Tools are provided and children are asked to solve problems and report their solutions. The teacher watches, listens, and questions until the solution strategy is understood.

ACTIVITIES

(At Least Forty-Five Minutes per Episode)

Materials: Videotapes V, VI, VII

If teachers have not seen the Introduction to CGI tape (Videotape I), it can be shown and discussed now. Next, selected episodes from Videotapes V–VII can be used. It should be kept in mind that the classroom scenes on the tapes are not intended to be viewed consecutively as they appear on the tapes. Participants should always be made aware that there are many ways to organize instruction in a CGI classroom and they should see several examples of each Big Idea. Although you will find certain points about each episode you wish to emphasize, the episodes below illustrate major points in Chapter 7. They may be helpful as you begin your work in a CGI Professional Development Program.

- How teachers pose problems and what they do while children are solving problems: Gehn (Videotape VII @ 32:25); Keith (Videotape V @ 16.50); Hawkins (Videotape V @ 0:00)
- Reasons for selecting problems: Keith episode and interview (Videotape V @ 16:50, 29:45)
- Use of tools: Falkner (Videotape VI @ 8:36); Kolan (Videotape V @ 36:09); Koberstein (Videotape VI @ 0:00)
- Listening and questioning children: Meyer (Videotape VII @ 21:21); Falkner (Videotape VI @ 8:36).

Viewing Classroom Episodes as a Group (At Least Forty-Five Minutes per Episode)

Materials: Videotapes V, VI, VII

The episodes can be viewed by the entire group and followed by general discussion. Small groups can then be given specific questions on which to focus (suggestions follow) as the episode is viewed again. Each group could then report on their question to the entire group.

- What kinds of problems did the teacher ask children to solve?
- What did the teacher learn about the children as they reported their solution strategies?
- What questions did the teacher ask to elicit children's solution strategies, and what did s/he find out?
- How did the teacher ensure that all children were solving appropriate problems?

Viewing Classroom Episodes in Small Groups (At Least Forty-Fives Minutes per Episode)

Materials: Videotapes V, VI, VII

Small groups can view the episodes and prepare to lead an entire group discussion on the following specific points:

- This is how this teacher works with his or her students, and this is how we would modify what s/he does.
- What problems did the teacher use to find out what her/his students knew about place value? What did s/he find out?
- What did teachers in [select episodes] do while the children solve problems?
- How did these two teachers [select two] take care of children's differences in ability to solve problems?

ASSIGNMENTS

Read Chapter 7 in *Children's Mathematics.*

REFLECTIONS ON TEACHING CHAPTER 8

"CGI Classrooms"

This chapter provides a vision of teaching in which each teacher uses his/her knowledge of children's thinking to create a unique mathematics program that includes broad instructional components identified in classrooms taught by expert CGI teachers. ***Providing some guidance while still leaving room for teachers to construct their own instructional practice requires a delicate balance of leadership.*** To assist in helping you achieve this balance, many classroom episodes are provided on Videotapes V–VII. The episodes vary by grade, classroom organization, teacher expertise and knowledge, problem types and content included, and sophistication of the children's solution strategies. As often as possible, teachers' own words are used to illustrate the critical points in interviews.

Because instructional maturity evolves over a long period of time, the major ideas in this chapter and the videotapes should be returned to often as participants and leaders mature in their CGI beliefs, knowledge, and experience.

BIG IDEAS

1. Teachers are not told specifically how to organize their classrooms, but common components of CGI classrooms are described.
2. In CGI classrooms, problem solving, which usually involves single- and multidigit word problems of the types studied in Chapters 1–6, is the basis of the curriculum.[1]
3. In CGI classrooms, children communicate their thinking about problems to the teacher and to each other.
4. Children come to understand mathematics as they solve many problems and construct relationships among mathematical ideas.
5. CGI teachers are actively involved in understanding their students' thinking and use that understanding as a basis for planning instruction.
6. CGI teachers believe that children can and should figure out ways to solve problems. Children learn important mathematical ideas when many problems are solved.

You are encouraged to become familiar with the episodes on Videotapes V–VII and select the ones that will be most helpful for your own situation. The following episodes are referenced here and will be helpful in many situations:

Videotape V: "Classrooms, Part 1"
  Yttri, kindergarten class @ 7:48

1. Nonroutine problems not discussed in Chapters 1–6 are often included in classrooms taught by expert CGI teachers. However, for beginning CGI teachers, understanding a more confined set of problems has been sufficient to enable them to begin organizing their classrooms around problem solving.

Keith, first/second-grade class @ 16:50
Kolan, second-grade class @ 36:09

Videotape VI: "Classrooms, Part 2"
Statz, third-grade class @ 19:55
Falkner, second-grade class @ 8:36

Videotape VII: "Classrooms, Part 3"
Meyer, kindergarten class @ 21:21

ACTIVITIES

You are encouraged to design your own procedures for using the classroom videos to help your participants learn about CGI. Usually the videotapes are used concurrently with Chapters 2–8. Listed in the videotape log is the content emphasized in each episode so episodes can be selected to match content under discussion. The specific activities listed below are suggestions to help you initiate your work.

Participating in Directed Small-Group Viewing of Videotapes (Time Varies)

Materials: Videotapes V–VII

There are several different ways to organize small-group viewing.

- In small groups, participants watch several episodes selected by you and then identify common elements. The groups' lists are then compared with each other and the list identified in Chapter 8.
- The participants are divided into small groups and then watch episodes selected by you. Each group is assigned a question to answer in relation to the episode watched. You may want to use the following sample questions.
  - How are problems posed in each episode?
  - What kinds of questions does each teacher ask to elicit children's thinking?
  - How is the class organized so that each child is able to report his/her thinking?
  - What kind of planning did the teacher do before class?
  - How do the problems relate to the knowledge and interests of the children in the class?
  - What does each teacher do to help students learn mathematics?

Selecting Problems Related to Specific Content (Time Varies)

Materials: Videotapes V–VII

In the following episodes, teachers are encouraging the development of multidigit ideas. Have participants identify the problems and how they relate to the development of understanding of problem solving with multidigit numbers. Have teachers record and classify children's strategies.

Hawkins, Grade 2: Videotape V @ 0:00
Koberstein, Grade 2: Videotape VI @ 0:00
Falkner, Grade 2: Videotape VI @ 8:36
Statz, Grade 3: Videotape VI @ 19:55

Assessing Knowledge and Use of Children's Thinking (At Least One Hour per Episode)

Materials: Videotapes V–VII

In the following interviews—which were filmed subsequent to each classroom episode—the teacher discusses what she knows about her children's thinking. With the participants, discuss what the teacher says, rewatch the classroom episode, and discuss what other information participants would consider if this had been their class.

Yttri, Videotape V @ 10:40
Keith, Videotape V @ 29:45
Koberstein, Videotape VI @ 3:51
Statz, Videotape VI @ 47:31

Visiting CGI Classes (Time Varies)

Help participants arrange schedules and substitute teachers so they can visit other beginning or expert CGI teachers as they teach. Time also should be arranged for discussing problems and successes with implementing CGI. It is helpful if participants identify specific focus issues, such as assessment or problem selection. Many other issues are likely to arise, so asking participants to come back to workshops with specific things to discuss can be helpful.

ASSIGNMENTS

Read Chapter 8 in *Children's Mathematics.*

APPENDIX A: SAMPLE WORKSHOP AGENDAS

These agendas are case examples of how two teams of leaders have taught CGI workshops. They are not intended to be prescriptive. They are intended to provide you with an idea of how topics can be sequenced and the typical pacing of a workshop.

WORKSHOP SAMPLE AGENDA A

(Two-Part, Five-Day Workshop, Break After Two Days)

Workshop Activities	*Facilitator Notes*
Day I	
Solving Nonstandard Problem	
Solve Roller Coaster problem from Intro tape. Each group solves two ways—stress that strategies should be different, even if answers are not. **Share** strategies. Discuss if second graders could do the problem. **Begin defining** Direct Modeling as "acting out the problem." (Definition will be refined throughout day.) **Watch** video of children solving the problem.	Direct Modeling is a powerful problem-solving tool that allows children and adults to solve what some would consider an Algebra problem. We want to encourage a sense-making approach to mathematics.
Ranking a Set of Problems	
Give teachers a list with JCU, Mult, Mdiv, Pdiv, CDU, and SRU problems (problems that Rachel solves on Videotape II work for this activity). **Ask** which problems would be harder or easier for a first grader to solve. Discuss rationale for ranking.	Elicit teachers' knowledge about problem difficulty. Begin discussion of differences and similarities between problems.

Workshop Activities	*Facilitator Notes*

Watching Rachel

Watch Rachel solve some of the problems discussed.
Discuss strategies. Note how the action in the problem dictates her actions with the blocks.

Continue defining Direct Modeling on chart paper (to be added to during day).

Children follow sequence of action in problem and represent sets with materials.

Practicing Direct Modeling

Have teachers solve JRU, JSU, JCU problems using Direct Modeling definition. This should raise questions about how a child would model a story without a start.
Continue discussion of what makes problems difficult.

Distinguish between manipulating materials and following time sequence. Direct Modeling is not about using manipulatives, but means that child is literally acting out the problem as if it were a story.
Experience with problem types will make distinctions between them clearer.

Building a Problem Type Chart

Distribute three join problems and three separate problems to teachers to categorize.
Discuss categorization. Distinguish between children's thinking categories and adults' thinking categories.
Distribute two PPW and CDU problems to teachers to categorize.
Discuss and develop problem type chart.

Kids use different strategies on problems.

Two major distinctions:
Action/No Action
Location of Unknown

Watching Rachel

Watch student solve other problems.
Identify problem type and discuss each strategy.
Alter Direct Modeling definition as needed.

Continued development of definition of Direct Modeling and of problem types.

Introduction to Counting and Derived Facts Strategies

Present a problem that children solve on Videotape II.
Invite teachers to use a strategy other than Direct Modeling.
Watch child solve problems and then discuss abstractions involved in Counting and Derived Facts.

Counting and Derived Facts strategies continue to follow action described in problem.

Watching Yttri and Hawkins Segments from Videotape V

Workshop Activities	Facilitator Notes
Ask teachers to identify problem type. **Pose question**: What did the teacher find out about her students' thinking?	Teachers can assess students in whole-class setting. They don't have to do individual interviews. Continue distinguishing between problems.

Assignments

Read Chapters 1–3.
Write a set of problems.

Day II

Opening Class

Workshop Activities	Facilitator Notes
Share problems written as assignment in small groups. **Choose** one to share with the whole group. **Share** problems discussing classification.	Practice with problem classification. Assess teachers' understanding of problem types by looking at problems they have written.

Practicing Identifying Problem Types

Workshop Activities	Facilitator Notes
Complete Problems to Be Identified (see Appendix B). (Some of these are difficult to categorize.) **Encourage** teachers to consider Direct Modeling strategies to help in differentiating problems.	Practice with problem classification. Reemphasize action in problem as focus of children's attention when solving problems.

Practicing Using Strategies

Workshop Activities	Facilitator Notes
Have the teachers solve a few examples from the worksheet using Direct Modeling, Counting, Derived Facts, and other strategies. **Share** strategies from CDU and JSU problems. Reemphasize differences among strategies and problem types.	Point out that children might rerepresent problem. Using manipulatives does not indicate a Direct Modeling strategy. The only Direct Modeling strategy for Start Unknown problems is trial and error, which requires the child to deal with the ambiguity of starting with "some."

Watching Gehn Segment from Videotape VI

Workshop Activities	Facilitator Notes
Ask teachers what type the problem is and how solution strategies of children differ.	Multiple solution strategies occur in classroom. Children at different levels can solve the same problem. Important feature of CGI classrooms is the *discussion* of strategies.

Workshop Activities	Facilitator Notes

Using a Solution Strategies Chart

Workshop Activities	Facilitator Notes
Introduce Solution Strategies Chart. **Watch** children solving problems on Videotape II. **Use** Solution Strategies Chart to identify strategy and level of development. **Hand out** Solution Strategies Chart.	Problem type and solution strategy need to be taken into account when assessing children's development.

Working with Multiplication/Division Problems

Workshop Activities	Facilitator Notes
Describe multiplication scenario. **Ask** teachers to write division problems and to direct model problems that go with scenario. **Share** problems.	Division problems will be modeled differently.

Preparing for Interview

Workshop Activities	Facilitator Notes
Distribute set of cards with one problem per card. **Discuss** order of problems for interview.	Interview should be tailored to child. A child's approach to problems should dictate which problems are given.

Interviewing Child with Partner

Workshop Activities	Facilitator Notes
One partner gives problems; the other records child's work.	Experience using problems to assess child's thinking.

Discussing Interviews

Workshop Activities	Facilitator Notes
Analyze child's development with partner. **Share** analysis with group. **Share** frustrations/successes with group.	Typically children can solve JRU, SRU, and Mult problems. This generally surprises teachers. Children who have not been in CGI classrooms are often not used to using manipulatives to solve problems. Teachers often discuss how they would introduce their students to using manipulatives. Children are not used to explaining their thinking. Teachers often talk about how they would facilitate discourse in their classrooms.

Assignments

Interview students.
Pose a JCU problem with the numbers 27, 51 to their students in a whole-group lesson.

Teachers have a two-week break between this portion of the workshop and the next.

Workshop Activities	*Facilitator Notes*

Day III

Matching the Problem Type

Distribute to each teacher a card with a problem on it.	Review problem types and solution strategies.
Find the other people who have the same problem type. (You should have four or five cards with JCU, SRU, SSU, CDU, Pdiv, and Mdiv. After groups have formed, each person should solve his/her problem using Direct Modeling, Counting, and Derived Fact.)	Get reacquainted with peers in class.

Examining Children's Strategies

Watch kids solving multiplication/division using more sophisticated strategies (#7, 8, 9, and 10 from Videotape III).	Examine abstractions children make to handle more complicated problems.
(Note: Victoria's strategy is particularly interesting and generates a lot of discussion.)	Note that advanced strategies are harder to use for partitive division.

Discussing Interview

Be explicit about what the child did, focusing on capabilities, not deficits. **Be able** to duplicate a strategy. **Be ready** to talk about what the strategy says about the child's thinking. **Discuss observations** in groups (split the class in half or into thirds).	Review solution strategies and levels of development.

Watching Garden Video

Solve problems from Garden video. **Pose** question for watching video: How does Ms. Garden handle the range of abilities in her class?	Begin discussion of classroom issues.

Organizing Small-Group Discussion

Describe how things went when you asked a group of children to solve problems. **Discuss** questions this raised for you and issues you'd like examined in workshop.	Look at practical experience and analyze issues involved in CGI instruction.

Workshop Activities	*Facilitator Notes*

Looking at Strategies Before and After

Watch clip #26 from Videotape IV. (Child uses algorithm incorrectly at start of year and has flexible strategy at end of year.) **Show** September portion of clip. **Characterize** child's base-ten understanding at the beginning of the year. (Why does child have trouble?) **Show** May portion. **Characterize** child's base-ten understanding at this point. (What has changed?)	Base-ten understanding emerges slowly. Algorithms are often misunderstood if taught before base-ten concepts develop.

Examining Existing Strategies for Developing Base-Ten Understanding

Discussion. In small groups, discuss the following questions: • What is base-ten understanding?	Access teachers' knowledge for developing base-ten knowledge.
• What tasks and activities do you use to facilitate its development? • What base-ten understanding did you see in the children in your class when you did the assignment?	Motivate discussion of problems that facilitate development.

Using Multiplication/Division Problems as Starting Points

Watch tape of Falkner and Koberstein. (One person at each table should focus on one child in the class on the tape. At the conclusion of the tape, the table should discuss each child and his or her base-ten understanding.)	Multiplication and Measurement Division problems with groups of ten promote base-ten understanding. Multiplication and division should not be delayed until third grade.

Day IV

Practicing Identifying Problem Types

Distribute multiplication/division problems. (Use some that will promote base-ten understanding.)	Problems that involve groups of ten encourage base-ten thinking.
Identify problem type and consider if problem will promote base-ten understanding.	Two-digit numbers measured into groups smaller than ten do not allow children to use tens.

Identifying Strategy Types

Workshop Activities	Facilitator Notes
Watch Videotape IV:	
Watch Kate.	Exposes teachers to multiple solution strategies.
Solve JRU (44,19) like Kate.	
Watch Joel. Did Joel solve it like Kate?	Encourages teachers to use invented algorithms.
Solve JRU (55,37) like Joel.	
Watch Laurel. Did Laurel use Joel's technique?	Frees them from the standard algorithm.
Solve next problem using Laurel's technique.	Focuses teachers' attention on differences among strategy types.
Watch next child. Did he/she use Laurel's technique?	
Watch more kids identifying strategy type if time allows.	

Watching Statz Segment from Videotape II

Discuss: How does a teacher build children's base-ten knowledge?
Discuss implementation issues.

Ranking Base-Ten Problems According to Difficulty

Workshop Activities	Facilitator Notes
Distribute set of 12 problems with different number combinations and problem types.	Decade numbers are easier for children than nondecade numbers.
Discuss: Which ones would be easier for a child to do in his/her head? What strategy is more likely to be used with each problem?	Problems that require regrouping are the hardest. Problem type potentially affects solution strategy.

Preparing for Interview

Write set of six problems to assess and build base-ten concepts.

Role-Playing Interview

Role-play. (Using set of problems just written, one person plays the child and one the interviewer. The child writes a brief synopsis of his/her base-ten understanding before the interview.) The "interviewer" tries to infer the items on the list based on the "child's" work.

Workshop Activities	*Facilitator Notes*

Day V

Solving Problems

Distribute problems: A third of the class is given the problem 306 – 179 as CDU, a third as JCU, and a third as SRU. **Solve** two ways using blocks, hundreds chart, and number line. **Compare** strategies by mixing up groups to form new groups so that new group has two people who solved CDU, two that solved JCU, and two that solved SRU. **Discuss** role of material, problem type, and notation in strategy use. **Share** longitudinal study results (Carpenter et al., 1998, see Appendix D).	Materials and problem type affect children's strategy use. There are a multitude of strategies for any one pair of numbers.

Using Notations

Show examples of children's written work. **Discuss** how children's use of notations develops in the classroom.	Children's understanding of symbols can emerge through problem solving rather than before problem solving.

Watching Keith Segment from Videotape V

Discuss: How does Ms. Keith nurture children's use of notations?

Looking for Commonalities Across CGI Classrooms

Generate list of features (in small groups) that were noticed in the classroom videos. **Create** class list.	CGI teachers as facilitators, listeners . . . CGI classrooms as places of communication, problem solving . . .

Closing Workshop

Write a personal plan for starting your journey into using CGI. **Share** ideas with grade-level group. **Discuss** as panel: Experienced CGI teachers answer questions about their own journey into using CGI. **Have** participants do evaluations.	Each teacher integrates CGI into his or her own style of teaching and uses it in ways that "make sense."

WORKSHOP SAMPLE AGENDA B

(Three-Part, Six-Day Workshop, Breaks Between Days Two and Three and Days Four and Five)

Day I

1. **Give overview.**
2. **Introduce informal strategies.** Participants solve the problem: "A minivan has 7 seats. If 19 children take the minivan to the zoo, how many children can sit 3 to a seat and how many have to sit 2 to a seat?"
   - Share solutions.
   - Watch a child solve this problem.
3. **Discuss**: What is CGI and how does it fit into current math education reform?
4. **Do journal activity**:
   - Write a half page about what one of your students knows about math.
5. **Do Ranking Problems activity** (described in Reflections on Chapter 1).
6. **Build** Problem Type Chart (described in Reflections on Chapter 2).
7. **Introduce** Multiplication and Division types (described in Reflections on Chapter 4).
8. **Do journal activity:**
   - Write about strategies other than Direct Modeling that a child could use to solve a Join (Change Unknown) and a Measurement Division Problem.
   - Share with group.
9. **Watch Videotape II** to introduce Direct Modeling, Counting, and Number Facts strategies.
10. **Write a set of problems** (one of each of the nineteen types) in small groups.

Day II

1. **Turn in problems** (leaders will review and hand back later). Choose a Join (Change Unknown) problem written by a participant, have participants find Direct Modeling, Counting, and Number Facts strategies.
2. **Practice identifying problems**. (See Appendix B: "Problems to Be Identified.")
3. **Watch** Meyer classroom episode (Videotape VII). Label each strategy. Discuss as group.
4. **Review strategies**. In small groups, generate Direct Modeling, Counting, and Number Facts strategies for a list of problems. (See Appendix B: "How Would Children Solve These Problems?")
5. **Discuss** and **build** Children's Solution Strategies Chart (see Reflections on Chapter 3).
6. **Watch** Rachel (Videotape II) solve a series of problems. Use Solution Strategies Chart to keep track of her strategies. Predict how she would solve problems not shown.
7. **Watch** CGI Intro tape (Videotape I).
8. **Do journal activity:**
   - What is CGI? Write some reflections in your journal.
9. **Conduct question and answer session.**

10. **Do journal activity (short):**
    - What is my plan for getting started with CGI?
    - Share with grade groups.
11. **Conduct question and answer session.**
12. **Assignments:**
    - Read Chapters 1, 2, 3, 4, and 5.
    - Interview a child.
    - Pose a Join (Change Unknown) problem with the numbers 27, 61 to a group of children and keep track of the different strategies.

Participants have a two-week break between this portion of the workshop and the next.

Day III

1. **Discuss:**
    - What have you tried?
    - Lead large-group discussion for a couple minutes, then divide into small grade-level groups.
2. **Watch** classroom videotapes to find common components of CGI classrooms: Mary Jo Yttri (Videotape V), Sue Gehn (Videotape VII), Therese Kolan (Videotape V). Stop briefly between tapes and discuss.
3. **Discuss (as a group):** Common components of CGI classrooms.
    - In small groups, make a list of common components and a list of differences between classes.
4. **Do journal activity:**
    - Write about what one of your students understands about mathematics. (This will be a child you will follow over the course of workshops.)
5. **Share** interviews from homework. Put people in pairs, have partners check each other's problem types, strategy names, and level. Have teachers talk together about what they wrote as a summary of what this child understands.
6. **Discuss** the interview process as a group. How did interviews go? What would you do differently? How could you find out more information? (Try to get teachers started on the idea of adjusting an interview to what a child does.)
7. **Role-play** (described in Reflections on Chapter 3).
8. **Conduct question and answer session.**

Day IV

1. **Share** results of giving common problem to children. Teachers meet in small groups of mixed grades. They come up with a range of strategies for these problems. They are asked to group similar strategies together. Before starting, they are told that strategies should vary in terms of what the child understands about base-ten.
2. **Give** examples of similar and different strategies with terms linked to their reading.
3. **Watch** episode #26 from Videotape IV. Discuss what this child understands about base-ten. Discuss standard algorithm.
4. **Do journal activity:**
    - Write about your goals for one of your students.
5. **Conduct question and answer session.**

6. **Evaluations.**
7. **Assignments:**
   - Read Chapters 6–9.
   - Interview three more children, keeping track of questions and strategies.
   - Write a summary for each child.

Teachers have a two-week break between this portion of the workshop and the next.

Day V

1. **Discuss** concerns.
2. **Review** base-ten strategies. Have participants generate solution strategies to three problems. Make sure they generate Direct Modeling With Tens and several Invented Algorithms.
3. **Discuss**: Base-ten number strategies. Show Videotape IV. Discuss individual children's strategies.
4. **Share** interviews in small groups.
5. **Discuss** (as a group): Did anyone adjust questions in their interviews as they went, based on what they learned about a child?
6. **Role-play** (described in Reflections on Chapter 6).
7. **Do journal activity:**
   - What is my plan for teaching children to solve problems with large numbers?

Day VI

1. **Do exploring different strategies with different problem types activity** (described in Reflections on Chapter 6).
2. **Discuss (as a group):** Discuss all the possible ways to solve 717 – 398. Do you see a relationship between problem type and strategy? Are some problem types more conducive to certain strategies? Do some problem types encourage certain base-ten understandings more than do others?
3. **Watch** Statz episode from Videotape VI.
4. **Discuss** instruction issues: What does an active CGI teacher do?
5. **Do journal activity:**
   - What does Ms. Statz do to help her students learn?
6. **Write** three questions you still have about CGI. Watch Intro tape (again). Did tape have suggestions for addressing this concern?
7. **Conduct question/answer session.**
8. **Evaluations.**

APPENDIX B: PROBLEMS AND WORKSHEETS

Rachel's Problems

Classification of Word Problems Chart

Classification of Word Problems Chart (Blank)

Problems To Be Identified: Sample Set

Problems To Be Identified: Sample Set (Responses)

How Would Children Solve These Problems?

Finding a Problem for a Strategy

Children's Solution Strategies Chart

Addition/Subtraction Relative Difficulty Worksheet

Addition/Subtraction Relative Difficulty Worksheet (Responses)

Multidigit Numbers Relative Difficulty Worksheet

Multidigit Numbers Relative Difficulty Worksheet (Responses)

Hundreds Chart

RACHEL'S PROBLEMS

From Videotape II:
"Children's Strategies for Addition/Subtraction"

1. Lucy has 8 fish. She wants to buy 5 more fish. How many fish would Lucy have then?

2. TJ had 13 chocolate chip cookies. At lunch she ate 5 of them. How many cookies did TJ have left?

3. Janelle has 7 trolls in her collection. How many more does she have to buy to have 11 trolls?

4. Max had some money. He spent $9.00 on a video game. Now he has $7.00 left. How much money did Max have to start with?

5. Willy has 12 crayons. Lucy has 7 crayons. How many more crayons does Willy have than Lucy?

6. 11 children were playing in the sandbox. Some children went home. There were 3 children still playing in the sandbox. How many children went home?

7. Rodney is having some kids over for jelly donuts. 7 donuts can fit on one plate. How many plates will Rodney need for 28 donuts?

8. Karina had 20 cupcakes. She put them into 4 boxes so that there were the same number of cupcakes in each box. How many cupcakes did Karina put in each box?

CLASSIFICATION OF WORD PROBLEMS CHART

Problem Type			
Join	*(Result Unknown)* Connie had 5 marbles. Juan gave her 8 more marbles. How many marbles does Connie have altogether?	*(Change Unknown)* Connie has 5 marbles. How many marbles does she need to have 13 marbles altogether?	*(Start Unknown)* Connie had some marbles. Juan gave her 5 more marbles. Now she has 13 marbles. How many marbles did Connie have to start with?
Separate	*(Result Unknown)* Connie had 13 marbles. She gave 5 to Juan. How many marbles does Connie have left?	*(Change Unknown)* Connie had 13 marbles. She gave some to Juan. Now she has 5 marbles left. How many marbles did Connie give to Juan?	*(Start Unknown)* Connie had some marbles. She gave 5 to Juan. Now she has 8 marbles left. How many marbles did Connie have to start with?
Part-Part-Whole	*(Whole Unknown)* Connie has 5 red marbles and 8 blue marbles. How many marbles does she have?	*(Part Unknown)* Connie has 13 marbles. 5 are red and the rest are blue. How many blue marbles does Connie have?	
Compare	*(Difference Unknown)* Connie has 13 marbles. Juan has 5 marbles. How many more marbles does Connie have than Juan?	*(Quantity Unknown)* Juan has 5 marbles. Connie has 8 more than Juan. How many marbles does Connie have?	*(Referent Unknown)* Connie has 13 marbles. She has 5 more marbles than Juan. How many marbles does Juan have?

CLASSIFICATION OF WORD PROBLEMS CHART (BLANK)

Problem Type			
Join	*(Result Unknown)*	*(Change Unknown)*	*(Start Unknown)*
Separate	*(Result Unknown)*	*(Change Unknown)*	*(Start Unknown)*
Part-Part-Whole	*(Whole Unknown)*	*(Part Unknown)*	
Compare	*(Difference Unknown)*	*(Compare Quantity Unknown)*	*(Referent Unknown)*

PROBLEMS TO BE IDENTIFIED: SAMPLE SET

1. Jabul folded 6 cranes. How many more cranes does he need to fold to have 10 cranes for the peace banner?
2. Albert has 4 children. Each child eats 1/2 an egg for breakfast. How many eggs do Albert's children eat at breakfast?
3. Christopher is playing a video game. He has collected 8 magic jelly beans. If an extra life costs 2 jelly beans, how many extra lives can Christopher buy?
4. Ms. Lee's class is going to the zoo. There are 30 children in Ms. Lee's class and 7 children can fit in one car. How many cars will Ms. Lee need to take her class to the zoo?
5. Some children put on a play for their parents. 5 children were rabbits, 2 were squirrels, and 8 were foxes. How many children were in the play?
6. 3 children were playing on the monkey bars. 8 more children ran over to play on the monkey bars with them. How many children were playing on the monkey bars then?
7. Lila has 10 cookies. She wants to share her cookies with 3 friends. How many cookies will each person get if Lila and her friends each get the same amount of cookies?
8. Ellen spent $5.28 for lunch today. Larry spent $11.12. How much more money did Larry spend for lunch than Ellen?
9. The national debt is $3,445,500,000,000. What's your share?
10. It takes 3/4 yard of cotton to make a T-shirt. How many T-shirts can be made with 4 yards of material?
11. James had a book of stickers in his desk. His mother gave him 22 more. He now has 36 stickers. How many stickers were in his book to start with?
12. Albert's cabbage patch has 4 rows of cabbage. In each row, there are 5 heads of cabbage. How many heads of cabbage does Albert have in all?
13. Lakesha has 29 animal crackers. Coreen has 15 animal crackers. How many more crackers does Lakesha have than Coreen?
14. Martha bought 6 T-shirts at Prange Way. She has 3 children. She would like to divide the T-shirts equally among her children. How many T-shirts does each child get?
15. There are 5 people on the Green Bay High track team. If a relay race is 150 meters long and all 5 team members participate, how far will each team member have to run?
16. There were 567 geese on the marsh. A bunch flew away. Now there are 150 geese left. How many geese flew away?

PROBLEMS TO BE IDENTIFIED: SAMPLE SET (RESPONSES)

1. JCU
2. Mult
3. Mdiv
4. Mdiv
5. PPW-WU (3 PARTS)
6. JRU
7. Pdiv
8. COMP-DU
9. Pdiv
10. Mdiv
11. JSU
12. Mult
13. COMP-DU
14. Pdiv
15. Pdiv
16. SCU

HOW WOULD CHILDREN SOLVE THESE PROBLEMS?

In the space provided, describe a specific strategy for each problem and general strategy type.

PROBLEM	PROBLEM TYPE	DIRECT MODELING STRATEGY	COUNTING STRATEGY	DERIVED FACTS STRATEGY	OTHER POSSIBLE STRATEGY
Laurie's mom will not let her have more than 13 cats. Patrick's 3-year-old cat is going to have kittens. Laurie has 6 cats. Patrick will give Laurie some cats for her birthday. How many cats would Laurie need to get for her birthday to have 13 cats altogether?					
Jennifer bought a box of new markers for school. At Thanksgiving time, Norma gave her 9 more markers. At the winter break she counted her markers. There were 17 of them. Jennifer is sure she didn't lose any markers at all. How many markers were in the new box she bought?					
Karen and Luke love to walk and look at birds. Karen walked 4 miles this weekend. Luke walked 12 miles this weekend. How many more miles did Luke walk than Karen?					
Kevin loves blocks. He made a tower of 14 green and blue blocks. The cat came along and knocked over part, but not all, of the tower. There were 6 blocks left in the tower. How many blocks did the cat knock over?					

FINDING A PROBLEM FOR A STRATEGY

Directions: Listed below are descriptions of strategies that children have used to solve problems. Assume that the children are using strategies that correspond to the structure of the problem posed to them. Decide which problem each child is solving; include the problem type and the numbers in the problem.

1. Kevin says, "9, 10, 11, 12, 13," and holds up a finger for each count after 9. He looks at his hand and says, "4, the answer is 4."

2. Janet draws seven lines as she counts, "1, 2, 3, 4, 5, 6, 7." She then leaves a space and draws six more lines as she counts, "8, 9, . . . 13." She looks at her drawing and counts the second set of lines. "1, 2, 3, 4, 5, 6, my answer is 6."

3. Eli counts out 16 cubes. She counts, "1, 2, 3 . . . 9" pulling one cube away from the group for each count. She then counts the remaining cubes, "1, 2, 3, . . . 7, my answer is 7."

4. Tory says, "12, 11, 10, 9, 8" and holds up a finger for each count after 12. He looks at his hand and says, "4, it is 4."

5. Anita says, "21, 22, 23, 24, 25" and holds up a finger for each count after 21. She says, "25, that is it, 25."

CHILDREN'S SOLUTION STRATEGIES CHART

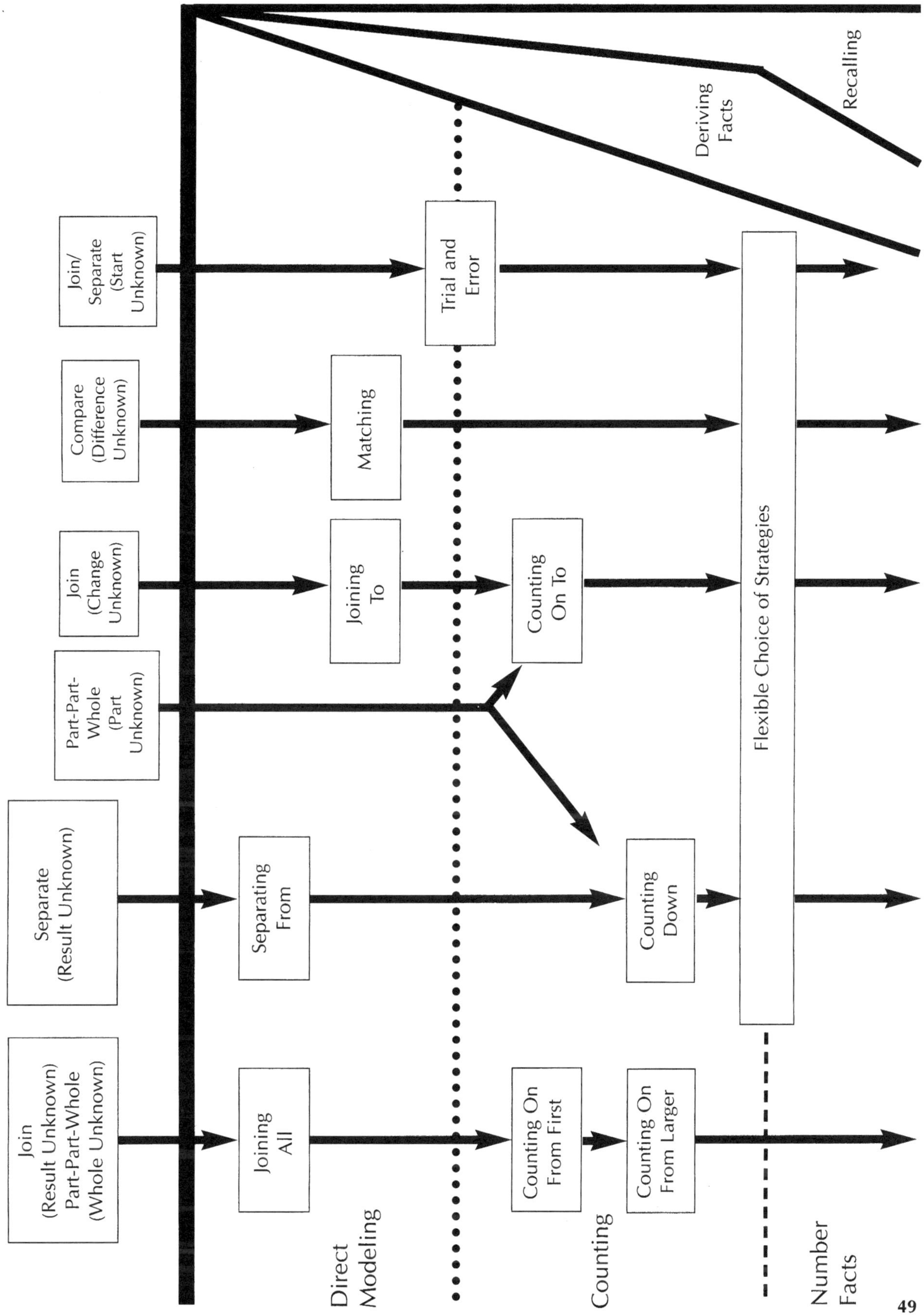

ADDITION/SUBTRACTION RELATIVE DIFFICULTY WORKSHEET

Directions: For each of the following pairs of problems, indicate which problem you think generally would be more difficult for first-grade students. Circle A if you think problem A is clearly more difficult than problem B. Circle B if you think problem B is clearly more difficult than problem A. Circle E if you think the problems are of approximately the same level of difficulty. Assume that the problems are read aloud to the children and reread as often as necessary so that reading ability is not a consideration. Also assume that the children have counters available, which they can use to help them solve the problem if they wish, and that they can take as long as necessary to solve the problem.

Problem A	**Problem B**
1. A B E Mary had 11 gumballs. She ate 4 gumballs. How many gumballs does Mary have left?	Justin had 11 cookies. He gave 4 cookies to Lynn. How many cookies does Justin have left?
2. A B E Myesha had 13 apples. She and her friends ate 5 of them. How many apples does Myesha have now?	Chris has 5 apples. How many more apples does Chris need to pick to have 13 apples all together?
3. A B E Mark had 12 fish. He gave 8 fish to Penny. How many fish does Mark have left?	Doug has 12 snakes. Jan has 8 snakes. How many more snakes does Doug have than Jan?
4. A B E Ann has 8 flowers. How many more flowers does Ann have to pick to have 12 flowers?	Mr. Smith has 12 dogs. 8 are big and the rest are little. How many little dogs does Mr. Smith have?
5. A B E There are 14 hats in the closet. 6 are red and the rest are green. How many green hats are in the closet?	14 birds were in a tree. 6 flew away. How many birds were left?
6. A B E Francis had 8 lollipops. His mother gave him 5 more lollipops. How many lollipops does he have now?	There are 8 girls and 5 boys on a soccer team. How many children are on the soccer team?
7. A B E Michelle had 12 candy bars. She gave 5 of them to John. How many candy bars does Michelle have left?	Adrien had some apples. She ate 5 of them. Now she has 7 apples left. How many apples did she have to start with?
8. A B E Nbip has 15 cookies. She eats 9 of them. How many cookies does she have left?	Kevin has 8 stickers. If he gets 9 more stickers how many stickers will he have then?

ADDITION/SUBTRACTION RELATIVE DIFFICULTY WORKSHEET (RESPONSES)

The following list gives the identification of each problem type on the worksheet and the relative difficulty for each pair.

Pair	Problem Type A	Problem Type B	More Difficult
1.	Separate (Result Unknown)	Separate (Result Unknown)	E
2.	Separate (Result Unknown)	Join (Change Unknown)	B
3.	Separate (Result Unknown)	Compare	B
4.	Join (Change Unknown)	Part-Part-Whole (Part Unknown)	B
5.	Part-Part-Whole (Part Unknown)	Separate (Result Unknown)	A
6.	Join (Result Unknown)	Part-Part-Whole (Whole Unknown)	E
7.	Separate (Result Unknown)	Separate (Start Unknown)	B
8.	Separate (Result Unknown)	Join (Result Unknown)	E

MULTIDIGIT NUMBERS RELATIVE DIFFICULTY WORKSHEET

Directions: For each pair of problems, decide which problem you think would be more difficult for a young child to solve. Circle the letter that corresponds to the more difficult problem. If you think the two problems are equally difficult, circle E. Write why you made the decision you did.

	Problem A	**Problem B**
1. A B E	Shannon had 45 baseball cards. She got 32 more baseball cards. How many did she have then?	Laura had 47 stickers. For her birthday, she got 35 more stickers. How many stickers did she have then?
2. A B E	Rico got 92 jelly beans. He ate 21 of them. How many jelly beans did he have left?	Susan had 42 rocks in her rock collection. She went to the lake and found 53 more rocks. How many rocks does she have in her collection now?
3. A B E	Kevin has 76 peanuts. He gave 58 of them to his mom. How many peanuts does Kevin have left?	Marlene has 7 bags of marbles with 10 marbles in each bag. She also has 6 extra marbles. How many marbles does she have?
4. A B E	Nicholas had 91 dollars. He spent 37 dollars on some new shoes. How much money does he have left?	Chris has 37 dollars. She got 54 dollars for her birthday. How much money does Chris have now?
5. A B E	Kyra drew 20 trolls. How many more trolls would she need to draw to have 85 trolls in her picture?	Duke collected 23 leaves. How many more leaves would he need to collect to have 80?
6. A B E	Lakita had 57 toy cars. She gave 23 of them to her sister. How many toy cars did she have left?	DeMarco had 63 hats. If he gives 27 of them away, how many will he have left?

MULTIDIGIT NUMBERS
RELATIVE DIFFICULTY WORKSHEET (RESPONSES)

1. Unless children are Direct Modeling by Ones, problem B, which requires regrouping, is more difficult than problem A.

2. Problems A and B are equally difficult, independent of strategy level.

3. Problem A is more difficult than problem B for children who Direct Model with Tens or who use invented algorithms. Problem B might be more difficult than problem A for children who Direct Model with Ones.

4. Problem A is more difficult than problem B for children who Direct Model with Tens or who use invented algorithms. Regrouping issues are more difficult when separating than when joining. Problems A and B are equally difficult for children who Direct Model with Ones.

5. Problem B is more difficult than problem A for children who Direct Model with Tens or who use invented algorithms. It is more difficult to deal with a nondecade starting number when Direct Modeling by Tens for a JCU than to deal with a nondecade ending number (try it and see). It is also more difficult to use invented algorithms when you have to start with a nondecade number rather than when you end with one.

6. Unless children are Direct Modeling by Ones, problem B, which requires regrouping, is more difficult than problem A.

HUNDREDS CHART

1	2	3	4	5	6	7	8	9	10
11	12	13	14	15	16	17	18	19	20
21	22	23	24	25	26	27	28	29	30
31	32	33	34	35	36	37	38	39	40
41	42	43	44	45	46	47	48	49	50
51	52	53	54	55	56	57	58	59	60
61	62	63	64	65	66	67	68	69	70
71	72	73	74	75	76	77	78	79	80
81	82	83	84	85	86	87	88	89	90
91	92	93	94	95	96	97	98	99	100

APPENDIX C: GETTING STARTED QUESTIONS

Over the years, we have worked with many teachers as they started using Cognitively Guided Instruction. Although we don't have answers as to how a teacher should use CGI, we have identified many questions, some of which are listed below. We do not provide answers to the questions. Instead, we refer to an instructional episode in one of the classroom videotapes for information that will encourage reflection about the question. Sometimes we provide quotations from teachers about the ways they have dealt with the issues raised in the questions.

How does a teacher ask good questions to find out what children are thinking and to help them?

> Almost any classroom tape or strategy tape
> Craig Meyer's class (Videotape VII @ 21:21)
> Ginny Koberstein's class (Videotape VI @ 0:00)

How does a teacher facilitate children's reporting of problem solutions?

> Kathy Statz's use of journals (Videotape VI @ 19:55)
> Annie Keith's questioning (Videotape V @ 16:50)

How does a teacher respond to incorrect solutions?

> Michelle Garden's class (Videotape VII @ 0:00)
> Almeta Hawkins' class (Videotape V @ 0:00)
> Kathy Statz's class (Videotape VI @ 19:55)
> Annie Keith's class (Videotape V @ 16:50)

How does a teacher help a child who can't get started solving a problem or who gets stuck?

> If a child is struggling and really has no idea where to begin I might . . . give them a starting place, like, "Why don't you start with these counters?" But I don't give them the strategies. (Susan Gehn, first- and third-grade teacher)

> Annie Keith's class and interview (Videotape V @ 16:50, 29:45)
> Therese Kolan's class (Videotape V @ 36:09)
> Michelle Garden's class and interview (Videotape VII @ 0:00, 14:18)

How does a teacher encourage children to move to more mature strategies?

> For example, I might see a kid using counters. I know that this kid could do this problem without using the counters. And I might encourage him

to do it without the counters. I would say, "Would you try this without any counters?" (Susan Gehn, first- and third-grade teacher)

Kathy Statz's class and interview (Videotape VI @ 19:55, 47:31)
Sue Gehn on Introduction to CGI tape (Videotape I @ 15:00)

How does a teacher get children to listen to other children?

Kathy Statz's class and interview (Videotape VI @ 19:55, 47:31)

How can a teacher encourage children to use invented algorithms?

I don't demonstrate strategies for using invented algorithms. I do encourage the kids. For example, if I have given a problem like "420 cookies plus 340 cookies—how many cookies are there altogether?" I might see a kid using counters, and if I know that this kid could do this without using the counters. I would say, "Would you try this without any counters?" I don't expect all the kids who are using invented strategies for numbers that are easier, like the decade numbers, to just be able to do it when there is regrouping involved. However, I do give those problems so that other children will share their strategies and how they have done the regrouping. I don't expect all kids to be doing invented strategies, but the kids who are can share with other kids, and that will help those kids. (Susan Gehn, first- and third-grade teacher)

Kathy Statz (Videotape VI @ 19:55)

How does a teacher meet the needs of diverse children?

When you really start looking at children, you see all the challenges, and they are there! To work with a diverse population, whether it's a child of color or children of [limited] economic means. You are going to have a HUGE diversity. You start saying, "How am I truly going to get that child, not this whole class?" But when you take each child and say what is best for that child, that is huge, and that keeps you intellectually stimulated. It keeps you going. It keeps you saying, "Okay, what do I need to do? How am I going to get this child to work up to her potential?" (Mazie Jenkins, first-grade teacher)

Kathy Statz's class (Videotape VI @ 19:55)
Michelle Garden's class (Videotape VII @ 0:00)

How does a teacher write story problems?

One day last week I spent . . . almost two hours where I had bought cookies for the classroom, and they had to find out how many cookies were in each package because I told them how many were in a row, how many rows, and they had to decide how many cookies there were all together and then how many cookies would each child get if I were to divide them up, and it took us the whole afternoon to do that problem. . . . (Susan Gehn, first- and third-grade teacher)

But now when we read books and stuff we will actually solve many problems related to what is in the book. Like today we were doing George Washington. Okay. When was he born? How many years ago would that be? I used to think that they couldn't figure it out so I would tell them. Now we actually sit and figure it out. Before I would have said, no, this is too difficult, they will never get it, and just pass it by. But I think because I am listening to the kids and I see what they are able to do, I am giving them the opportunity to figure it out by themselves. . . . You know, as long as we are reading a book, let's solve some problems that are in the book and actually sort of blend it all together. (Mazie Jenkins, first-grade teacher)

Michelle Garden's class (Videotape VII @ 0:00)

What does a teacher do while children solve problems?

Almeta Hawkins' class (Videotape V @ 0:00)
Ginny Koberstein's class (Videotape VI @ 0:00)

What about textbooks?

I don't use a textbook any more. I am responsible for the objectives that our district has set down, but I know these objectives and so I just go about teaching them in a different way, plus I get all those objectives down in about nine weeks of school, and then I just go on. (Susan Gehn, first- and third-grade teacher)

How do I get started?

Almeta Hawkins' class (Videotape V @ 0:00)
Mary Jo Yttri's class (Videotape V @ 7:48)

APPENDIX D: SELECTED ANNOTATED BIBLIOGRAPHY

More than ninety articles have been written about Cognitively Guided Instruction. What follows are summaries of thirteen articles that cover a variety of issues addressed in our writing. It is important for people who teach workshops to be familiar with CGI research. We recommend that you read these articles before teaching a workshop. These articles will also be useful to the teachers in your workshop who want more information about CGI. The journals and books should be available in any university library. Please contact our office if you have trouble locating an article.[1]

Carey, D. A., E. Fennema, T. P. Carpenter, and M. L. Franke. 1995. "Equity and Mathematics Education." In *New Directions in Equity for Mathematics Education*, edited by W. Secada, E. Fennema, and L. Byrd. New York: Teachers College Press.

Research on equity in mathematics education and research on children's thinking are blended and discussed in this article. Cognitively Guided Instruction is presented as a program that helps teachers move toward equitable mathematics instruction. Examples from a group of teachers who worked with disadvantaged children in the Washington, DC, area are presented. The authors discuss examples of teacher change and classroom instruction.

Carpenter, T. P., E. Ansell, M. L. Franke, E. Fennema, and L. Weisbeck. 1993. "Models of Problem Solving: A Study of Kindergarten Children's Problem-Solving Processes." *Journal for Research in Mathematics Education* 24 (5): 427–440.

Kindergarten children from CGI classes were asked to solve a variety of story problems in individual interviews. Seventy percent of the children used a correct strategy to solve a Partitive Division problem; seventy-three percent of the children used a correct strategy to solve a Measurement Division problem; and sixty-seven percent of the children used a correct strategy to solve a two-step Multiplication and Subtraction problem. Other results are described in the paper.

Carpenter, T. P., E. Fennema, and M. L. Franke. 1996. "Cognitively Guided Instruction: A Knowledge Base for Reform in Primary Mathematics Instruction." *Elementary School Journal* 97 (1): 3–20.

This paper addresses how understanding children's thinking can provide coherence to teachers' pedagogical content knowledge and their knowledge of subject matter, curriculum, and pedagogy. This paper also describes how chil-

1. Complete publication list available from Wisconsin Center for Education Research, 1025 West Johnson Street, University of Wisconsin–Madison, Madison, WI 53706.

dren's abstract symbolic procedures can be thought of as progressive abstractions from their Direct Modeling solutions.

Carpenter, T. P., E. Fennema, P. L. Peterson, C. P. Chiang, and M. Loef. 1989. "Using Knowledge of Children's Mathematics Thinking in Classroom Teaching: An Experimental Study." *American Educational Research Journal* 26 (4): 499–531.

The authors provide a detailed description of the first CGI study, in which twenty control teachers were compared to twenty teachers who had attended a CGI workshop. Differences among their classes in terms of teachers' knowledge, teachers' beliefs, classroom practices, and student achievement are described.

Carpenter, T. P., M. L. Franke, V. Jacobs, and E. Fennema. 1998. "A Longitudinal Study of Invention and Understanding in Children's Multidigit Addition and Subtraction." *Journal for Research in Mathematics Education* 29: 3–20.

A group of approximately sixty children were followed over three years as they progressed from first through third grade in CGI classrooms. Children were interviewed at the end of each year. The different paths that children followed in learning more sophisticated strategies are described.

Empson, S. B. 1995. "Research into Practice: Using Equal Sharing Situations to Help Children Learn Fractions." *Teaching Children Mathematics* 2 (2): 110–114.

What we know about learning and teaching fractions in a CGI class is presented in this paper. It was written for teachers and contains many interesting examples and suggestions for getting started with teaching fractions.

Fennema, E., T. P. Carpenter, M. L. Franke, and D. A. Carey. 1992. "Learning to Use Children's Mathematics Thinking: A Case Study." In *Schools, Mathematics, and the World of Reality*, edited by R. Davis and C. Maher. Needham Heights, MA: Allyn and Bacon.

This article describes a case study of a teacher as she learned to use CGI in her mathematics instruction. How this teacher changed and the stages she passed through as she changed are described.

Fennema, E., T. P. Carpenter, M. L. Franke, L. Levi, V. Jacobs, and S. Empson. 1996. "A Longitudinal Study of Learning to Use Children's Thinking in Mathematics Instruction." *Journal for Research in Mathematics Education* 27 (4): 403–434.

The authors provide a detailed report of the second CGI study, which followed a group of teachers and children over three years as the teachers learned to use CGI in their mathematics instruction. How teachers changed over these years and the stages they passed through in learning to use CGI are described. Their students' achievement is also described.

Fennema, E., M. L. Franke, T. P. Carpenter, and D. A. Carey. 1993. "Using Children's Knowledge in Instruction." *American Educational Research Journal* 30 (3): 555–583.

This article describes a case study of one CGI teacher and her students. What happened in this teacher's class, what this teacher knew and believed about learning mathematics, and what her students learned is described. This paper has a good section on the background and philosophy of CGI.

Franke, M. L., and D. A. Carey. 1997. "Young Children's Perceptions of Mathematics in Problem-Solving Environments." *Journal for Research in Mathematics Education* 28 (1): 8–25.

Children from CGI classes were interviewed to determine their beliefs about learning mathematics. These children believed that mathematics was an open-ended, problem-solving endeavor where communicating their ideas was important. Children valued a variety of solution strategies and did not think that speed and accuracy were what determined success in mathematics.

Hankes, J. E. 1994. "Building on the Math Knowledge of Disadvantaged Learners: An Alternative to Basic Skills Remediation." *Arithmetic Teacher* 2 (8): 452–458.

CGI is presented as an example of a program that can help teachers situate their mathematics instruction in meaningful contexts, which can thus help disadvantaged learners. This paper was written for teachers and has many real-life examples.

Jenkins, M., L. Lehman, J. Maas, B. Marten, K. Wells, and P. Wood. 1991. *Good Books, Good Math: Integrating Multicultural Literature and Mathematics Problem Solving*. Madison, WI: Madison Metropolitan School District.

This book contains thirty-six sets of story problems. Each set was written to go with a different children's book. All books contain a multicultural theme. To obtain a copy of this book, send $7.00 to Cathy Caro-Bruce, Madison Metropolitan School District, The Teachers' Workshop, 545 West Dayton Street, Madison, WI 53703 (608-266-6456).

Viadero, D. 1995. "It All Adds Up." *Education Week* (March): 33.

This article was written for a nationwide newspaper aimed at education administrators and policymakers. An overview of CGI and descriptions of classes are presented. This article gives a good beginning idea of what CGI is all about.